"This is a fascinating and comprehensive book about the history of ghosts and the supernatural, a history that most modern-day ghost hunters tend to neglect. Brian Righi has delved into man's long obsession with the unknown in a way that makes for compelling reading and reinforces the idea that hauntings are created by the events of the past and that there is much for us to learn from the events that have gone before. Highly recommended for every ghost enthusiast's bookshelf!"

—Troy Taylor, author and founder
of the American Ghost Society

"Prepare to experience shivers when you follow Brian Righi along shadowy corridors of dark, forbidding haunts in his book, *Ghosts, Apparitions, and Poltergeists: An Exploration of the Supernatural through History*."

—Dr. Dave Oester, www.ghostweb.com

"Brian Righi, an experienced paranormal investigator, has produced a highly readable history of the supernatural as manifested across a wide range of cultures, from earliest times to the present. He also offers sound advice to psychical researchers on how to conduct an investigation and what equipment to take. The result is very enjoyable, packed with useful information and good sense."

—Dr. Tom Ruffles, author of
Ghost Images: Cinema of the Afterlife

"A good mix of history, theory, and practicality with just enough spooky anecdotal accounts thrown in to make it of interest to the storytelling crowd. An excellent primer for the serious ghost-hunter wannabe, and an invaluable addition to any bookshelf."

—Jeff Danelek, author of *The Case for Ghosts*

"In *Ghosts, Apparitions and Poltergeists,* Brian Righi offers a clear and concise presentation of ghostly encounters that not only validate his own experiences, but also encompasses their historical significance. He uncovers ghostly phenomena ranging from ancient Sumeria to the modern world with an inquiring mind, wit, and knowledge of the occult. This book is a must-read for ghost hunters, and in fact anyone who has ever had an eerie, inexplicable experience with the paranormal."

—Melba Goodwyn, author of *Ghost Worlds*

Ghosts,
Apparitions
and
Poltergeists

Angela Conley

About the Author

Brian Righi graduated from DePaul University in Chicago and is the author of numerous books on ghosts and the paranormal. He developed an early love for the topic while traveling through Europe with his parents and continues even today to crisscross the United States, investigating tales of the supernatural and lecturing on his experiences. He currently calls Texas his home, where he lives with his beautiful wife Angela and his favorite cocker spaniel, Madison.

GHOSTS, APPARITIONS AND POLTERGEISTS

Brian Righi

An Exploration of the
Supernatural through History

Llewellyn Publications
Woodbury, Minnesota

First Edition
First Printing, 2008

Cover design by Lisa Novak
Cover image © Radius Images/Punchstock
Editing by Lee Lewis Walsh
Interior book design by Joanna Willis

Llewellyn is a registered trademark of Llewellyn Worldwide, Ltd.

Library of Congress Cataloging-in-Publication Data
Righi, Brian, 1972–
   Ghosts, apparitions, and poltergeists : an exploration of the supernatural through history / Brian Righi.—1st ed.
       p. cm.
Includes bibliographical references.
   ISBN 978-0-7387-1363-2
   1. Ghosts—History. 2. Apparitions—History. 3. Poltergeists—History.
I. Title.
   BF1461.R53 2008
   133.109—dc22

                                                        2008021697

Llewellyn Publications
A Division of Llewellyn Worldwide, Ltd.
2143 Wooddale Drive, Dept. 978-0-7387-1363-2
Woodbury, MN 55125-2989, U.S.A.
www.llewellyn.com

Printed in the United States of America

To my beloved Angela,
for putting up with me and my ghosts.

CONTENTS

Acknowledgments

Writing a book of this magnitude is certainly not a solitary pursuit and, although only one name ends up on the spine, it really is an effort born from the sweat of many individuals. Having said that, I want to take the time to thank a few of the people who made this book possible. Many thanks to Bill Krause, Vanessa Wright, Karl Anderson, and the wonderful staff at Llewellyn Publishing for believing in the project. Also to Robert Larson for allowing me the time to write when I should have been working. To Carl Hullett and Les Ramsdell, two intrepid ghost hunters who took me under their wings and showed me the ropes. Finally, let us not forget all of the ghost hunters, mediums, theologians, and madmen who came before us and made this field what it is today.

INTRODUCTION

Like many in this rather unusual field of research, I first became interested in psychic phenomena at a very early age, a fact for which I happily blame my parents. I can remember as a young child sitting around the kitchen table at night with friends and family, as they sipped their strong-smelling coffee, and listening to my parents recount their experience of living in a haunted house in Germany. Each night I would sit glued to the edge of my seat, wide-eyed and terrified as tales of sinister ghosts returning after a tragic end filled my ears. Later that night, after all the guests had left and my parents tucked me into bed, the initial thrill and excitement of those stories began to wear off. Then every floorboard's creak or rattling shutter was transformed by my imagination into the midnight ramblings of the scariest ghosts and monsters that ever lurked about a house. Under my bed, skeletons waited for the chance to snatch at my feet, while the closet housed the most ill-assorted collection of demons ever seen. Although I lost a lot of sleep at that age, I never lost my desire to hear more of the stories.

It was with this spirit that, at the age of thirteen, I was fully intent on spending the night in a real haunted house in hopes of encountering a ghost of my very own. At that time there sat an old, dilapidated farmhouse on the edge of Miller's Pond, which every kid in the neighborhood knew was haunted. And why not? Weren't all old, shabby, dark houses sitting empty on the edge of murky ponds haunted? In fact, local legend held that the house was home to not one, but two gruesome spirits. A vague tale—no less embellished as it passed from one kid to another—recounted the tragic story of two young lovers who, when told they could no longer see one another, committed suicide in the house. It was said the boy hung himself in the attic over the separation and, when the girl heard of his death, she flung herself into the pond and drowned. Reports circulated among the kids on my block that late at night strange lights were seen in the abandoned structure, and if a kid were brave enough to enter the house at night, he would come face to face with the ghostly lovers. The perfect haunted house!

With such tales in our heads, I set out one night with several other young ghost hunters, without our parents' knowledge (parents never really know what their kids are up to), and approached the house that sat on the edge of Miller's Pond. Filled with the excitement and fear of our first ghost hunt, we were fully intent on capturing a real ghost, even if we had no idea in the world how such a thing was to be accomplished. Tentatively we made our way into the house and through its maze of dusty rooms. The moon rested high in the night sky and its beams lit the broken glass of the house's windows, playing tricks on our eyes. Did something just move in the darkened corner behind us? What was that noise in the ceiling above?

Now I'd like to say that on that night we captured our very first ghost and became instant celebrities, but the truth of the matter is, at the first sound of a creaking board, we ran out of there as if the devil himself were chasing us. To this day I still haven't captured a ghost or become a celebrity, but I have developed a love for ghost stories, which over the years has led me to other dark houses and moonlit cemeteries.

The purpose of this book is to introduce the reader to the fascinating world of ghosts. We'll begin the journey with a look back at the ghost lore of our early ancestors and follow the history of the subject all the way to the Spiritualist movement of the nineteenth century. From there we'll delve deeper into the theories about apparitions, ghosts, and poltergeists, listening to stories about them and critically examining their differences and similarities. Then finally, just when you thought the harrowing trip was nearing its end, we'll spend time with some of the greatest ghost hunters ever to walk a haunted house and learn how to conduct a ghost hunt of our own.

Ghosts, Apparitions, and Poltergeists: An Exploration of the Supernatural through History is sure to have something for everyone. It can be read as either a technical manual for the aspiring ghost hunter or as a collection of scary tales for pure enjoyment. What this book will not do is prove to you beyond a shadow of a doubt that ghosts do or do not exist. That will be for you to decide. So sit back and enjoy this book, but I warn you—you may find yourself sleeping with the lights on tonight.

Happy hunting.

Chapter 1

DIGGING UP
THE BONES

It is perhaps particularly appropriate that one who is about
to make a journey to the next world should look fully into
the matter, and tell stories about what we suppose to be the
nature of our residence there and after all, how else could
we spend the time until sunset?

— PLATO

he British Museum stood alone in the night and shrouded itself from the rest of London by a dense fog that rolled off the banks of the Thames River. George Smith, an assistant in the Oriental Department, sat at his tiny desk surrounded by mountains of antiquated books and crumbling clay tablets. By the dim light of a lone gas lamp, he squinted at the strange cuneiform writing before him and continued scribbling notes with growing excitement. He knew he had chanced upon a marvelous discovery when, that night in 1871, he translated an ancient Sumerian text, later known as the *Epic of Gilgamesh*, which contained one of the very first accounts of man's belief in the afterlife and one of the very first ghost stories ever written down.

Gilgamesh is the story of a Hercules-like character that roams the land slaying fierce demons and performing seemingly impossible feats of strength and cunning. Modeled after a Sumerian king of the early dynastic period (ca. 2700–2500 BCE), the legend was recorded on twelve clay tablets found in the ruins of the royal library in the ancient city of Nineveh. Gilgamesh, after many dangerous adventures, loses his friend and warrior companion Enkidu during a quest into the dark underworld of the spirits. Lamenting the tragedy, he turns to the gods for help, who eventually agree to one last meeting between the two friends. A hole is then opened at the feet of Gilgamesh, allowing the ghost of Enkidu to rise from the underworld and describe for his friend what awaited a Sumerian after his or her death. At first, Enkidu is reluctant to speak of the horrors faced by a spirit in the underworld, but eventually overcomes his hesitation with the warning to our hero that "if I must tell you what I have seen in the underworld, sit down and weep."

This passage is thought to be the first written evidence that our ancestors believed that beyond their everyday world of toil and struggle there existed another, darker place, inhabited by the souls of the dead. For the ancient Sumerians, the underworld was a place of weeping and darkness, where the spirits of both the good and the evil alike were punished. A dismal thought to look forward to in one's old age, but the Sumerians did allow one saving grace, as Enkidu explains when he continues his speech:

"Have you seen the spirit of the one who has no one left alive to love him?"

"I have," replied Gilgamesh.

"He eats the leftovers from the pot, the scraps of bread thrown into the gutter, things not even a dead dog would eat."

To the Sumerians, a man's fate after death was ultimately tied to the conduct of his living relatives. If they performed the proper magical formulas, prayers, and ceremonial offerings for the spirit of the deceased, then the trials and tribulations of the underworld could be made a little more bearable.

However, if a person died and left no living descendents to conduct the proper rituals, then only an eternity of pain and loneliness awaited him.

Throughout the history of many cultures, there has existed an apprehension about how the spirits of the dead were affected by the daily rituals of the living. The cosmic outlook of early man was one in which the worlds of the living and the dead were deeply intertwined. The Greeks, for example, were terribly afraid of dying without a proper burial. They believed that when a person died, his or her spirit began the perilous journey into the underworld. Money was placed in the mouth of a corpse at the funeral so that the departing spirit could pay Charon the Ferryman to take it across the River Styx. Foods such as pudding and cheese were placed on the body so that the traveling spirit could propitiate the three-headed monster Cerberus who guarded the entrance to Hades. If these needs were not met, the spirit could not enter into the next world and would be doomed to wander the earth, causing havoc among the living. To ensure that the spirits were sent on their way, the Greeks developed practices centered on the proper disposal of the body after death. For instance, in Athens there was a law stating that if a traveler came across a dead body, whether it be that of a friend or stranger, he was to cast dirt upon it three times. If he failed to do this, he was then required to travel to the nearest temple and conduct the appropriate sacrifices to the gods in order to expiate his sins. In the end, if a traveler neglected to do either, he could be subject to a stiff government fine. Greek sailors also bought a bit of afterlife insurance by tying a small reward to their body when they went to sea, in the hope that if they drowned and their body washed ashore, anyone finding it would have payment for giving them a proper burial.

Of equal concern to the Greeks was the need for the body to be buried within its native soil. If a Greek died far from his homeland, it was thought that his spirit would be unable to find its way back. Trapped in a foreign land, the spirit could not be properly cared for by its living descendents and would be subject to the misery of loneliness and aimless wandering. If a person did have the misfortune of dying far from home, his or her friends and family would gather and sing solemn invocations to the deceased person's soul in the hope that, by hearing this, the spirit would be comforted and find its way back. If a body could not be produced for burial because it was lost at sea or captured in battle, then a funeral was conducted all the same, with ceremonies and an empty bier as if the body were present. The hope was that a token burial was better than no burial at all.

Another culture that went to great lengths to prepare its dead for the journey to the afterlife was that of the Egyptians. To an Egyptian, death was not the end, but a brief interruption in a life that would continue elsewhere much the same as it had before. Life and death were like the Nile River and the deserts that surrounded it, constant and unchanging. When a person died, food, furniture, clothing, jewels, and even animals were buried with him or her. This would sustain the spirit in the next life and ensure that nothing would change.

More important, however, was the preparation of the body after death. The Egyptians believed that one component of the spiritual force that remained was called the *ba*, which relied on the body of the deceased for its existence. The *ba* was thought to be able to take on any shape it wanted and leave the tomb, returning to its body at night for rest. In scenes painted on tomb walls, the *ba* is shown as a bird with a human head, hovering over its entombed body. This required that great lengths be taken to ensure the preservation of the body after death, and so began the art of mummification.

When a person died, his or her body was first turned over to the temple priests in the *wabt*, or "place of embalming," who began the grisly task of preparing the body. First, small iron hooks were inserted through the nasal cavity to rip out chunks of brain matter. The abdomen was then cut open, and the stomach, liver, lungs, and intestines were removed, cleaned, and stored in small jars to be buried with the body. The heart, oddly enough, was left in place because it was thought to be the center of knowledge and will— something that made up the personality of the person and so would be needed in the next life. Finally, the body was washed with a mixture of pounded herbs, such as myrrh and cassia, and palm wine before being stored in natrum, a type of salt, for forty days. Then the body was wrapped from head to toe in strips of linen glued with gum and placed with all its possessions in a tomb. The entire process was carried out with solemn devotion, and each step was accompanied by various magical spells to help the deceased in the next life.

Besides the intricate preparations some cultures made in burying their dead, others maintained strong ties with the dead long after the funeral. The Romans, who held many beliefs in common with the Greeks, celebrated their funerals with public displays that were held by torchlight at night. During these ceremonies, singers would exclaim the praises of the deceased to the tunes of flutes, while actors staged important scenes from the deceased's life. The Romans left food at the tombs of dead relatives so that their spirits could eat, and would sometimes even bury them in their own homes so that they could better be looked after. In the Roman pantheon of spirits, *Lares* were considered good spirits and were invited into homes and towns to act as guardians. Most families had their very own *Lares*, composed of deceased relatives, who if treated properly could be called upon to protect the family in times of need.

This concern over the well-being of the dead stemmed from the belief that the spirits required the same things as the living. For instance, in Central and East Africa, it is still believed by some tribes that when the dead are tired of wandering in the jungle, they will come to someone they know and ask that person to build them a home. When this happens, the person is obligated to assemble the women of the village together at night to sing and dance for the spirit. The next day the village goes to the grave of the *obambo* (ghost) and makes a crude idol representing the dead person. This idol, along with some dust from the ground and the bamboo poles that carried the body to the grave, is brought to a small hut erected next to the house of the person the spirit visited. A white cloth is draped across the door of the hut and the spirit is then thought to reside there, helping anyone who leaves an offering of food.

Caring for the spirits of the dead by leaving offerings of food and other necessities can be found in the customs of many cultures the world over. The Pacific Islanders were known to watch a corpse for seven days following a death to make sure the devil did not come to visit and steal the body away. During this time, the dead person's bed and meals were prepared for him at home in case his wandering spirit grew hungry or tired. Similar traditions exist even today, although we may hardly realize their origins. Christmas, for example, is a time when children delight in leaving milk and cookies for Saint Nick, just in case the jolly old fat man gets hungry delivering all those toys. As innocent as this may seem, however, it is an ancient practice that first began in Ireland when family spirits returning home for Christmas Eve were rewarded with cups of milk left on the windowsill.

Another means by which our ancestors sought to appease wandering spirits of the dead and ensure their happiness in the next world was to hold a public festival in their honor. In late February and early March, the Greeks held what was called the Anthestria. Meals were provided in each home and the spirits were invited for dinner. Once they were thought to have eaten their fill, the family would ask them to leave again for one full year, practically guaranteeing a spirit-free home until the next festival. However, if these public displays and offerings to the spirits weren't observed appropriately or with the proper reverence, there could be dire consequences that would bring harm and even death to the people. The Roman poet Ovid once wrote of a town that had failed to observe the customary feast and offer gifts of fruits, salt, corn, wine, and violets to the *Manes* (ghosts from the underworld). Because of the transgression he recounts that "the injured spirits revenged themselves on the living and the city was encircled with the funeral fires of their victims. The townsfolk heard their grandsires complaining in the quiet hours of the night, and told each other how the unsubstantial troop of monstrous specters rising from their tombs shrieked along the city streets and up and down the fields."

In many Spanish-speaking countries, as well as the southwestern United States, people celebrate what is called *el Día de los Muertos*—the Day of the Dead. On November 1, altars are built in the family home and adorned with religious icons, special breads, and other foods for the dead. Church services are held and prayers offered for all those who have passed away, after which the graves of loved ones are cleaned and decorated. Picnics, parades, and other festivities follow. The human skeleton or skull is the main symbol of the celebration and decorates everything from candy sugar skulls to skeleton toys performing daily tasks such as dancing or playing musical instruments.

Similar to this is our own festival of Halloween, which has been practiced in the United States since the days of the early colonists. Every October 31, children dress up as ghosts, witches, and any number of horrific monsters. Scampering from house to house, they squeal "trick or treat" as they extend their bags to receive handfuls of goodies. Children are not the only ones partaking in this celebration, and adults enjoy the occasion by dressing up to attend costume parties, handing out candy, or turning their homes into one-night haunted houses complete with sound effects and monsters that pop out of the darkness.

Halloween or All Hallows Eve dates back to the Celtic festival of Samhain. For one night, the gates to the land of the dead were open and the barrier between the living and the dead was lifted. During Samhain, huge bonfires were set to light the way for the spirits of the dead, and food offerings were left for their journey. The Celts ritualized the event by dressing as the spirits or wild beasts they associated with their gods. Yet the event encompassed more than just the return of the dead; it also meant bringing in the harvests, slaughtering animals for winter, and the beginning of the dark half of the year. This was a time when winter approached and the long sleep of the land under its snowy blanket seemed to be a sort of death in itself.

After Christian missionaries reached the British Isles, the festival began to change. A common practice of the early church was to incorporate native customs into a Christian worldview. Pagan practices were adapted, consecrated, and renamed to fit the teachings of the church. Such was the case with the celebration of All Saints Day on November 1, to commemorate those saints that did not have their own feast days to be remembered by. November 2 was named All Souls Day, and was a day of recognition for those that had passed away during the previous year. Further weakening the original intent, the custom of dressing up as the wild and untamed pagan gods became distorted to encompass all the things the Christians feared most, including a long list of demons, witches, and ghosts. It was, after all, a time when the barrier between the living and the dead was at its thinnest, a time when the devil and his minions were given free rein to cause terror upon the earth.

Intricate burial rituals, festivals honoring the dead, and prayers for the departed served one basic purpose—to keep the dead in their graves. Man, both modern and ancient, has tempered his curiosity about the spirit world with a good dose of fear, which in turn has led to some rather colorful ways of dealing with returning ghosts. For instance, some believed that if a person died violently or before his appointed time, his ghost could return to seek its revenge on the living. One of the more common taboos about ghosts related to the proper way to bury those accused of murder or suicide. In the British Isles, authoritative decrees prohibited graveyard gates from being opened to these types of burials. However, there were exceptions. If the family persisted enough, or had enough money and influence, then the body could be allowed in under two conditions: the first was that the casket had to be carried over the wall and not through the gate, and the second was that the funeral had to be held at night when no one could witness it.

Tradition once held that such unfortunates were buried at a secluded crossroads with a stake driven through the heart. The stake would keep them from rising and harming anyone, while the crossroads location was an added precaution. If a restless spirit did rise, it might become confused as to which way to go and therefore couldn't return home to haunt those who had just given the deceased a rather unceremonious burial. In Denmark, returning spirits were so feared that before burial the big toes of a corpse were tied together to hobble the spirit, pennies were placed on the eyes to blind it, and scissors were left on the stomach, opened in the form of a cross, to prevent evil. Before the burial, nothing in the house could be moved in a circular pattern or it might upset the dead, and when the time for burial did come, the coffin would be carried out feet first, so that the spirit could not find its way back.

Even the innocent victims of violence were thought to be able to return seeking vengeance for the wrong done to them. The Norwegians feared one type of ghost more than any other—the *utbrud*, meaning "child carried out." In Norway, when a child was born unwanted or in a time of famine and couldn't be cared for, it was carried out into the cold, dark forest and left to die of exposure. Many thought the child's ghost could return and seek its vengeance on the living. Lone travelers passing through some quiet wood or marsh at night were often the prey of the *utbrud*. Being pursued by one, travelers could only save themselves by splashing into a stream or pulling out a knife, as *utbrud* were thought to fear only water and sharp metal blades.

Usually, however, returning spirits were believed to be tied to their place of death or burial as if drawn back to the scene of their tragedy and sorrow. Graveyards were feared and avoided, especially on nights when the moon was full and the mist covered the tombstones in ghostly vapors. Times like these were ripe for spirits and imaginations. As early as the fourth century BCE, the philosopher Plato wrote in the dialogue *Phaedo* a warning against lingering around tombs where the dead still lurked, because "it haunts, as men say, monuments and tombs; by these have been seen shadowy forms of souls, apparitions such as souls of this kind provide when they are separated from the body." In New Zealand, among the Kaffirs and Maoris, the hut where a person died was so feared it was considered taboo and deserted. No one was allowed to approach it and many times it was even burned down. In some instances, a spirit was so feared that the entire village was abandoned.

———•·•———

From man's earliest time, he appears to have lived with the notion that he was surrounded by a spirit world with which he could interact. At times this notion was embraced, at other times it was feared, and in some cultures we find a strange mix of both. If we were to list the varying spiritual beliefs of every culture throughout history (a task too large for any one book), we would find the common theme that the living and the dead were connected through ritual, superstition, and prayer. The ancient ruins of Nineveh with their crumbling tablets and timeworn tales of ghosts may seem a long way off, but their message continues to echo through to the present day. After death, something exists, and sometimes it comes back. Several years after George Smith translated the *Epic of Gilgamesh*, he set out alone on an expedition to the ruins of Nineveh. Sometime later, his fever-racked body was found in the desert along the way, and after being taken to the British Consul's home in Aleppo, Syria, he died; perhaps this is a warning of the dangers to be faced for those who dig too deeply.

Chapter 2

A WITCH'S BREW

Eye of newt, and toe of frog,
Wool of bat, and tongue of dog,
Adder's fork, and blind-worm's sting,
Lizard's leg, and owlet's wing,
For a charm of powerful trouble,
Like a hell-broth boil and bubble.

— WILLIAM SHAKESPEARE, *Macbeth*

*T*hroughout history there have been those who have claimed the ability or power to pierce the barrier that existed between this world and the next in order to communicate with the spirits of the dead. They were called by a host of names—priest, shaman, necromancer, witch, and medium, among others—but what they were called and who was chosen was dependent upon the time period and the culture in which they lived. Some were appointed into a type of priesthood, others were born into a particular caste devoted to the practice, and still others claimed they possessed a particular ability or talent that allowed them to act as a conduit or channel to the spirits. The latter often worked without the "blessing" of the society around them and so found themselves persecuted and exiled by neighbors who deemed the practice of speaking with the dead an evil trade.

One of the first documented cases of mediumship is found in the Old Testament book of 1 Samuel (28:7–16). King Saul, on the eve of a battle with King Achish and the Philistines, sought the help of a necromancer, known as the Witch of Endor, to raise the spirit of the prophet Samuel and seek his help in the coming battle. One night Saul turned to one of his attendants and said, "Find me a woman who is a medium, so I may go and inquire of her."

"There is one in Endor," the attendant said.

So Saul disguised himself, putting on other clothes, and at night he and two men went to the woman. "Consult a spirit for me," he said, "and bring up for me the one I name."

But the woman said to him, "Surely you know what Saul has done. He has cut off the mediums and the spiritists from the land. Why have you set a trap for my life to bring about my death?"

Saul swore to her by the Lord, "As surely as the Lord lives you will not be punished for this."

Then the woman asked, "Whom shall I bring up for you?"

"Bring up Samuel," he said.

When the woman saw Samuel, she cried out at the top of her voice and said to Saul, "Why have you deceived me? You are Saul!"

The king said to her, "Don't be afraid. What do you see?"

The woman said, "I see a spirit coming out of the ground."

"What does he look like?" he asked.

"An old man wearing a robe is coming up," she said.

Then Saul knew it was Samuel, and he bowed down and prostrated himself with his face to the ground.

Samuel said to Saul, "Why have you disturbed me by bringing me up?"

Unfortunately for the king, Samuel refused to help and foretold the death of Saul and his sons the next day in battle. Because Saul had outlawed necromancy in the kingdom of Israel, he had to disguise himself and visit the witch only under the cover of night. For the law of the land was the Law of Moses, which forbade necromancy and witchcraft, a law that was clear on the point: "There shall not be found among you ... anyone who practices divination, a soothsayer, or an augur, or a sorcerer, or a charmer, or a medium, or a wizard, or a necromancer for whosoever does these things is an abomination to the Lord" (Deuteronomy 18:10–13). The penalty for being caught practicing any one of these dark arts included the pronouncement that a "man or woman that hath a familiar spirit or that is a wizard shall be stoned to death" (Leviticus 20:27). Consorting with the dead, to the Hebrews, was an evil practice that darkened a man's soul and infected society with its evil. It was therefore not tolerated.

The Romans, on the other hand, held spiritual beliefs borrowed from their Greek cousins. Not only was there a lack of disdain for necromancers, witches, and other mediums, but in many cases they were relied upon to help determine matters both big and small. In the first century CE, the Roman poet Lucan writes in the *Pharsalia* VI of a young man determined to know his future at any cost. One day Sextus Pompey, the son of Julius Caesar's chief adviser, sought out the help of a horrid Thessalian witch named Erichtho. But before the witch opened the future to young Sextus, she warned him that although she could tell the future through her necromancy, she could not change it. Sextus, determined as ever, quickly agreed and the witch began her dark ritual.

First it was necessary to prepare herself, and to do this Lucan writes that she lived in an open grave surrounded by the corpses of the dead. The first thing she required was a freshly deceased body, which Sextus seemed to procure easily enough. She then passed a long metal hook through the corpse's jaw and roughly dragged it over rocks and stones until she reached a particular cave. In the inky blackness of the cave's interior lay a fissure that was thought to drop to Hades itself. Wrapping herself in a magical robe and a wreath of vipers, she cut a hole in the chest of the corpse. Into this she poured the foulest concoction imaginable— the froth of a mad dog, the marrow of a stag fed only on serpents, and the hump of a corpse-fed hyena.

When the body had been prepared in this manner, the witch began a horrendous chanting that seemed to mingle the barking of dogs and the howling of wolves, the screech of an owl, the roaring of wild beasts, the hissing of snakes, the crash of waves on rocks, the murmur of forest trees, and the bellow of thunder. Finally, the apparition of the dead man appeared but refused to enter the body. It could only be lured in after the witch threatened it with all the infernal powers that existed and with the promise that, at the conclusion of the ceremony, the body would be burned to ensure it was never used for this purpose again. The ghost then entered the body, which sprang up and answered all of Sextus Pompey's questions.

We don't know what questions Sextus asked or what replies were given, only that his life would not be recorded as a successful one. Some time later he wound up on the losing side when he opposed Julius Caesar's successor Augustus and he remained a hunted outlaw for the rest of his life.

The Greek system of communicating with the dead was much more organized and nowhere near as gruesome. In every major city across Greece, there was an oracle and a priesthood that, for a price, would divine the future for a person. Although each oracle differed in the method it chose to foretell events, one located in the city of Ephyra was particularly interesting. It was thought not only to be the site where the entrance to Hades was located, but also a place where the living could speak directly to the dead. A person wishing to have his future foretold would journey to the temple and, after presenting the proper gifts, write the question he wished answered on a piece of clay, which was then given to the priest. Once through the temple doors, however, there was no turning back from an ordeal that would last for twenty-nine days. The seeker would have to enter the underworld, a strange place of darkness and dreams, of dimming torches and hypnotic chanting, a place of the dead.

A priest chanting magical prayers would lead the supplicant down a long dark corridor into a small room. Left here, the supplicant would smoke hashish to experience mystical revelations through his dreams, and subside on mussels, beans, and pork, foods associated with the dead. Many days would pass, but in the underground passages of the temple there was only one long night without end. After an unknown period of time, a priest would enter and the person would receive the ritual cleansing of a steaming hot bath followed by an ice-cold drenching. Then, taking the man by the arm, the priest would lead him down another corridor, deeper into the underworld's blackness. Given a stone, the supplicant would throw it behind him in order to ward off any harm that followed and ensure his safety through the corridors. The end of this passage led to a great labyrinth of small rooms that the seeker passed through until he was completely bewildered and confused. Eventually he reached a hole in the ground, the legendary entrance to Hades where the souls of the dead waited.

Having entered the underworld, eaten the food of the dead, and seen many strange visions within its dark nightmare realm, the supplicant had reached the twenty-ninth day of his journey—the day the dead would speak. The supplicant would pour the blood from sacrificed animals into the hole to be drunk by the souls of the dead, allowing them to regain consciousness in order to foretell the future. Then, rows of priests would file in, chanting hypnotically the magical words to raise the dead. From the darkness of the ceiling above, a large cauldron would descend and remain suspended above them. At this point, an apparition would appear from the cauldron and answer the seeker's question. However, the answer the apparition would give was always in a cryptic verse that required the recipient to decipher its true meaning. Afterward, the supplicant would be purified with sulfur fumes and led out into the blinding sunlight of the world above. He had traveled through the underworld, spoken with the dead, and survived.

The ritual practice of raising spirits in order to foretell the future or solicit advice was important to many early cultures, but as the centuries wore on, this cult of the dead faced an enemy far greater than all the legions of Rome: the Christian church. In the West, the fledgling church of Christ was coming into its own. No more were only the slaves and peasants looking forward to a better life in heaven. Now kings and emperors were bowing to this new, unstoppable power—a power built on the Law of Moses, a power that would accept no other gods before it. Constantine the Great became the first Christian emperor and enacted a general prohibition against the oracles. Throughout the empire, the church proclaimed that the power of oracles, witches, and necromancers came from Satan. In 319 CE, Emperor Constantine persecuted diviners with the decree that "a soothsayer who approaches his neighbor's house is to be burnt; anyone inviting him, whether by persuasion or by money reward, is to be deprived of his goods and banished to an island" (Bettenson 1954, 26).

The battle for the hearts and minds of the people shifted back and forth until about the seventh century, when the church became the primary authority in the West. However, to its shame, this battle was not fought with the rhetoric of debate or the truth of one system over another, but with fire and sword. Untold numbers were killed over the centuries, many of them innocents. The few remaining practitioners of the old ways faded into the shadows as the Christians tore down their oracles and replaced them with churches. As a fitting epitaph to the conquest, one of the last verses uttered by the oracle at Delphi was recorded as, "The fountains are silent; the voice is stilled." This voice would remain only the hint of a whisper until one day, in a new land, it would begin to shout—or rather, to knock.

Chapter 3

"HERE,
MR. SPLITFOOT"

Knock three times on the ceiling if you want me . . .
— TONY ORLANDO AND DAWN

*I*t was a quiet winter's night in 1847. Outside the small wooden house in Hydesville, New York, the snow was settling across the landscape in drifting mounds. John and Margaret Fox had just finished tucking in their two daughters, Kate and Margaret, for the night. It had been a long day and the only thing they could think of now was retiring to the warmth of their own bed. There was little sound about the house at this late hour, the wind blowing against the windowpanes, the occasional pop and hiss of the fire, and then a new sound added itself to the others. A strange thumping began that seemed to come from the ceiling above the girls' room, a rapping noise with a rhythm that seemed almost intentional. Perplexed, John searched diligently for the source of the noise but could find nothing. Finally he gave up for the night and the couple retired to bed, hoping that the morning would bring some relief from the phantom knocking. By sunrise it had stopped, and the family members went about their day, reluctant to discuss what their Methodist preacher would have called "the workings of the devil." The day passed, and as bedtime approached, the Foxes looked forward to a night of peace and quiet— and that's when the knocking began again. Each night the knocking repeated itself, and no matter how hard the family searched for the source of the noise, each night they were left without explanation. For three months the knocking continued without a possible source being discovered.

On the night of March 31, 1848, Kate and Margaret were still awake, listening to the knocking and obviously unafraid, when they devised a game. Kate snapped her fingers and called out "Here, Mr. Splitfoot, do as I do." The girls often referred to the knocking as "Mr. Splitfoot," which at the time was a common nickname for the devil. This time, however, the knocks answered back by mimicking Kate's snapping.

Much to John and Margaret's dismay, word began to spread concerning the strange happenings at the Fox home. People from all over came to hear the knocks for themselves and soon the Fox family was inundated with curiosity seekers. Always willing to entertain their inquisitive visitors, the Fox sisters developed a code in order to communicate with what they claimed was a ghost. The system worked like this: the girls would call out questions and the spirit would respond by knocking once for "yes" and twice for "no." Mr. Splitfoot was also capable of rapping out the number of years a person was in age or the number of fingers a person held up.

In time the system grew to include letters of the alphabet and, with this more complex system of communication, the spirit began fleshing out an identity of its own. Through the coded knocks it claimed to be the ghost of Charles B. Rosma, a peddler who supposedly had been murdered when the former resident of the house, John C. Bell, a blacksmith, slit his throat with a butcher knife. It claimed Bell took five hundred dollars and the peddler's box before burying the body in the cellar. The next day the basement was dug up, but no body was found and John Bell denied any knowledge of or involvement in such a crime. Nor would the authorities investigate the matter further—after all, no one even knew if the murder had really occurred.

The crowds that descended on the Fox home, eager to see the two sisters, began to make life unbearable for the family. It was decided that the two sisters should be split up and sent to live with relatives. Kate went to live with their older, married brother, David, while Margaret went to live with their sister Leah Fish, a widowed music teacher. At this point, critics of the Hydesville haunting (and there are many) claim that with the separation of the sisters, the knocking stopped. Supporters, however, maintain that not only did the knocking continue, it developed into a full-blown haunting.

Regardless of the happenings back at the homestead in Hydesville, the sisters began communicating with various other spirits at their new homes. They would often invite people over for sittings, what Margaret called "spirit circles," and which later became known as séances. In 1849, during one of these spirit circles, Margaret claimed to receive a message from one of the spirits telling her that the time was right to hold a public demonstration of their powers and enlighten the masses as to the existence of an afterlife. Based on this otherworldly advice, the sisters rented the Corinthian Auditorium and charged spectators one dollar apiece. During the show, they allowed a committee of audience members to observe them closely and give a report to the overcrowded hall afterward. The committee concluded at the end of the show that they had no idea as to how the knocks were manifesting.

Suddenly a star was born—or rather three stars, because after their sister Leah witnessed all the attention Kate and Margaret received, she also developed the ability to communicate with the spirit world via rapping. So with Leah as their new manager, Kate and Margaret began touring the United States, demonstrating their uncanny powers. They held sittings for some of the most important figures of their time, including Mary Todd Lincoln, James Fenimore Cooper, and Harriet Beecher Stowe. For a time they even gave exhibitions at P. T. Barnum's museum.

In January 1850, Margaret allowed a committee of doctors to examine her over the course of several sittings. What they discovered, interestingly enough, was that although they could not account for how the knocks were being manifested, the sounds could not be produced if Margaret's legs were held tightly together while sitting. But the report put out by the committee did little to diminish the fame of the sisters. Instead, their popularity grew, and oddly enough, so did the phenomena they exhibited during their sittings. New sounds were added to their repertoire and they even convinced the spirits to materialize for their audiences.

The spark was lit, and the Fox sisters popularized the beginnings of a movement in the United States known as Spiritualism. Now common folk began meeting in darkened rooms across the nation, attempting to conjure the spirits of the dead. Everyone from socialites, to con artists, to housewives came out of the woodwork claiming mediumistic abilities. Yet the Fox sisters cannot take all the credit or all the blame (depending on your view). In the 1800s, the United States was ripe with independent religious thought, and earlier mesmeric demonstrators who went into trances and diagnosed diseases paved the way for the Spiritualists. The Christian church, with its reactionary views, came to see the movement as an infectious disease and struck back with denunciations both from the pulpit and in the papers. The *Olive Branch*, a Methodist paper published in Boston on June 19, 1850, quoted a Catholic source as saying:

> "Our readers ... will hardly believe that this delusion has so spread over New England, and towns in other states of New England origin, that scarcely a village can be found which is not infected with it. In most small towns, several families are possessed, the mediums between erratic ghosts and the crazy fool being, in some cases, a weak half-witted woman, but in most instances, a little girl, whom her parents and friends have prostituted to this wicked trade."

It seemed as though the long-dead enemy of the church had raised itself back to life and was enjoying fertile ground in a country thirsting for a sense of spiritual identity. The various denominations of American Christianity promised all the wonderful trappings of an afterlife, but the attractiveness of Spiritualism lay in its promise to *prove* an afterlife, complete with floating spirits.

The debate over Spiritualism prompted early scientists to investigate claims of mediumship and attempt to prove or disprove the validity of mediums. Many were opposed to the fantastical nature of the subject and set out with a vengeance to discredit the movement. The great Harry Houdini, for instance, besides being a world famous escape artist, spent a great deal of time exposing various mediums as fakes. Others had a genuine interest in discovering the true nature of the phenomenon and helped found what would later become known as the science of parapsychology. In addition to being studied by doctors and lay committees, the Fox sisters were observed by prominent scientist William Crookes under strict laboratory conditions. Crookes was not only unable to find any traces of fakery, but became convinced of the reality of the sisters' powers. Commenting on their legendary spirit knocking, he stated: "It seemed only necessary for her to place her hand on any substance for loud thuds to be heard in it, like a triple pulsation, sometimes loud enough to be heard several rooms off. In this manner I have heard them in a living tree, on a sheet of glass, on a stretched iron wire, on stretched membrane ... moreover actual contact is not always necessary; I have heard these sounds proceeding from the floor, walls, etc., when the medium's hands and feet were held" (Crookes 1972, 113). Crookes continued to study other supposed mediums and eventually came under fire for what many considered a glaring naiveté. The issue had become a three-sided fight between the allure and popularity of the Spiritualists, the fear and traditions of the church, and the logic and tools of science.

The powers of the Fox sisters were questioned again when, on April 17, 1851, a relative of the Fox sisters, Norma Culver, told the *New York Tribune* that Kate had confessed to her that she made the rapping noises herself by cracking the joints of her toes. Both sisters denied this, however, and continued to enjoy celebrity status until the late 1880s. Although still in demand, the Fox sisters' personal lives were by then in shambles as they suffered through divorce and alcoholism. On September 24, 1888, Margaret admitted to the New York Herald that she and her sister Kate were frauds. One month later, on October 21, she described to the New York World how she and Kate had started the knocking with an apple tied to a string in order to frighten their mother. Later, when crowds began flocking to their home, they were too frightened to admit their little joke and so began producing the sounds by cracking their joints. During their spirit circles, their sister Leah furnished information to them about the people they were sitting for, which they passed off as otherworldly revelations. To further prove the hoax, the sisters took the stage at the New York Academy of Music and demonstrated to the packed house just how they faked the rappings.

These admissions would lead one to think that the Fox sisters were through and that their hoax might even topple the Spiritualist movement. However, this couldn't have been further from the truth; those involved in the movement, and even the public at large, simply refused to believe that it was all untrue. Supporters of the movement claimed the sisters were paid or even coerced into these damaging testimonies by the Catholic Church, or that the ravages of alcoholism clouded their minds. Whatever their reasons, two years later, hungry again for the spotlight, the sisters recanted their earlier confessions and returned to the séance table. But they never regained the fame that they once enjoyed, and died impoverished in the 1890s.

The Spiritualist movement did not remain simply an American phenomenon. Like a pebble thrown into a pond, its rings of influence spread ever wider. From Hydesville it spread to New York, then to London, Cuba, and South America, eventually reaching as far away as Turkey.

Although the Fox sisters are certainly considered pioneers in the Spiritualist movement, the award for the most exciting medium of the 1800s would have to go to Daniel Dunglas Home. This Scottish-born American traveled Europe demonstrating amazing powers during séances, which included everything from materializing spirits to causing inanimate objects to move on their own. In 1855, he established what would later become known as the Browning Circle at the residence of John Rymer, a wealthy London solicitor. Prominent among the many famous Londoners that attended this informal gathering were writers Robert Browning and Elizabeth Barrett Browning.

Home likened himself to something of an ambassador for the otherworld and traveled about as the continual houseguest of several rich patrons. True, he never charged for a séance, but neither did he shy from accepting gifts or donations. Home's séances at the Rymer house were typical of the time. The sitting was held in a dimly lit room where the guests gathered. First, Rymer's dead child Watt would make himself known by speaking through Home while in a trance. After Watt's departure, any doubters present were asked to leave before the spirits would agree to come forward. With these obstacles out of the way, the show could begin—and what a show it was. Furniture moved, thumping was heard, musical instruments played by themselves, and the dead rose up and appeared before stunned onlookers. Home's most extraordinary feat during a séance occurred at Ashley Place in 1868, when he levitated out one window and into another in front of three witnesses.

<hr />

With the luxury of looking back on the past, how then are we to judge these spirit communicators, these mediums? They did stand much to gain in the form of fame, fortune, or even just a little excitement, and the history of the movement was replete with instances that would cause a rational person to doubt. The Fox sisters admitted they were frauds, proved how they did it, and then recanted the entire confession. D. D. Home was often accused of trickery, and although his exploits were widely circulated by the press and taken as fact by the English populace, very few people ever actually witnessed them. Even the witnesses to his famous levitation gave testimonies containing many discrepancies. Can we then dismiss these as elaborate parlor tricks used to take advantage of gullible individuals, or does every so often a small event occur that has no rational explanation, which causes us to hesitate before passing judgment? On November 23, 1904, the *Rochester Democrat and Chronicle* reported that in a small wooden house in Hydesville, a cellar wall collapsed, revealing the skeletal remains of a human corpse. The house was once owned by the Fox family.

Chapter 4

TALKING BOARDS
AND
GHOSTLY GOO

It's just a game—isn't it?
— PARKER BROTHERS

*T*he Spiritualist movement, which developed in the late 1800s, continues even to this day. In Western society, despite the fact that it prides itself on rational and scientific thought, one has only to turn to the back of any major magazine to find advertisements that promise some powerful medium will answer all of life's questions over the phone for a new low price. Some mediums are even successful enough to have their own television shows and spend an hour each day delivering messages from the Great Beyond. The mediums of today, like the necromancers of old, use many diverse means of communicating with the spirits of the dead. A few of the most important methods and their phenomena will be touched upon in this chapter, but remember that with a "science" as old as man and a religion as diverse as all the cultures of the world, we can only scratch the surface.

SPIRIT RAPPING

Spirit rapping manifests itself as tapping, thumping, bumping, and banging from a discarnate source. These sounds have been heard on walls, furniture, glass, trees, and even

people. In volume, they can be as faint as a tick or as loud as
an explosive crash. Curiously, although they may sound dev-
astating, they never seem to leave a mark on an object, even
though it may sound as if the object itself should have been
destroyed. Additionally, the rhythm or pattern of these raps
is distinctive to the communicating intelligence and varies
from case to case.

Considered one of the simplest forms of spirit communication, the phenomenon made its way into print for the
first time in the ninth century in the manuscript *Rudolf of
Fulda*, which recounted instances of communication with a
rapping intelligence. Yet in a time when plagues and wars
stalked the land and death seemed an everyday occurrence,
spirit rappings were considered an omen of coming death
and were known as *pulsatio mortuorum*. Any household experiencing these ghostly knocks on dark, moonless nights
could be assured that death would soon come to claim one
of their number. Not even the early church was immune
and church fathers named the rapping spirits *spiritus percu-
tiens*, which they banished from medieval Catholic churches
with special formulas at their benediction.

It wasn't until the late 1800s that rapping reached its peak
in what would become known as the "Rochester knockings,"
when the Fox sisters developed a code of knocks to communicate with a rapping spirit as previously discussed. Since
that time, rapping has become a mainstay at most séances.
A simple method requiring no special props other than the
cooperation of the spirit itself, rapping is also one of the easiest phenomena to fake. Some, like the Fox sisters, pulled it

off by simply cracking the joints of their toes, while others went to even greater lengths to fool their audiences. Mechanical devices used to produce the sounds could be hidden in the shoes or clothes of a medium. One such means was accomplished by hiding an electrical device in the heel of a medium's shoe and running a small thread from the device, up through the clothes, and into the sleeve. During the séance, the medium could work the thread into his or her hand and, with a simple tug of the string: *voilà!* Instant knocks from the spirit world.

TABLE TILTING

Also known as typtology, table tilting is the phenomenon that occurs when a spirit moves, shakes, or rattles a table as a sign of its presence. Also an early form of spirit communication, its first description is handed down to us by Ammianus Marcellinus in fourth-century Rome. Marcellinus describes a table cut from a large slab of stone, upon which were engraved the letters of the alphabet. Above the table, a cord was suspended, at the end of which hung a metal ring. Questions were posed to the spirits and the answer would be spelled out as the ring swung to the letters on the table.

Table tilting in its modern form sprang into use after the "Rochester knockings," much the same as spirit rapping did. Part of its popularity rested on the fact that anyone with a table could do it without the need for a professional and sometimes expensive medium. People would gather in the parlor and seat themselves around a small table. After the lights had been dimmed to make the room more inviting for spirits, the sitters would place the palms of their hands lightly on the table's surface. A question would be asked of the spirits, who would rattle the table in response. Sometimes the answers would come as mere tremors in the table, while at other times it would bang about violently or even levitate off the floor.

Table tilting became so popular in its heyday that doctors and scientists thought the craze dangerous to the public's mental health. In reaction, a committee was formed to study the fad, which it reported on in the *Medical Times and Gazette* on June 11, 1853. After heated debate, the committee's findings concluded that table tilting was due to the unconscious muscular activity of the sitters and not to any real spiritual presence. Scientist Michael Faraday tested sitters by placing their hands atop a flat surface, which rested on metal rollers. Any unconscious movements by the muscles in the palms of the hands could then be detected by the table's movement and measured. Not to be outdone by the scientific community, the church also rallied against table tilting, claiming it to be the work of Satan.

TALKING BOARDS

A talking board is a simple device: a board that has the letters of the alphabet, the numbers zero through nine, and the words "yes" and "no" printed on it. Questioners place their fingertips lightly on a pointer known as a planchette and then, after addressing a question aloud to the spirits, allow the pointer to move about the board from letter to letter, spelling out a response. Although used in ancient China before the birth of Confucius and by the Greek philosopher and mathematician Pythagoras in the fourth and fifth century BCE, this method of spirit communication did not become popular until an American, Elijah J. Bond, constructed a modern version in 1890. His device was called a "Ouija board." The name is a combination of the French and German words for yes, *oui* and *ja* respectively. It became all the rage after the First World War as many turned to the board as a means of dealing with the loss of their loved ones; you can now find it on the shelves of toy stores next to Scrabble and Monopoly. Bond's Ouija board was bought by Parker Brothers in 1966 and was marketed with playful, catchy phrases like, "It's just a game—isn't it?"

In the history of talking boards, many strange communications have been recorded from the spirit world, but none as prolonged or as highly contended as that of Patience Worth. Pearl Curran was a simple housewife from St. Louis who had dropped out of school at the age of fourteen. On the night of July 8, 1913, while playing with a Ouija board, a spirit calling itself Patience Worth spelled out an introduction and the two became fast friends. Patience claimed to be the spirit of a woman born in Dorsetshire, England, in 1649. Unmarried and of a poor family, she sought a new life in the American Colonies across the Atlantic. Unfortunately, the opportunities she sought eluded her, and after reaching the shores of the New World she was killed by marauding Indians.

Patience, it seemed, had a great deal more to say and was soon dictating poems, short stories, plays, allegories, epigrams, and historical novels. In the first five years of their literary partnership, Patience and Pearl produced over four million words. The most popular of these works was a three hundred thousand-word epic novel about the life of Jesus Christ entitled *The Sorry Tale*. Once published, these works provoked reactions that ranged from the enthusiastic to the skeptical. Those who believed in the authenticity of the writings asked how an uneducated person could produce works as well written and historically correct as these. Scholars, on the other hand, noticed a major discrepancy that could not be overlooked. Patience communicated in a form of late medieval English that had ceased to be used in the thirteenth century—four hundred years before Patience claimed to have been born.

Communication between Pearl and Patience continued over the course of nearly twenty-five years, although its quality began to deteriorate somewhat after about 1922. Many believe that changes in Pearl's life, including the deaths of her husband and mother as well as the birth of her first child at age thirty-nine, may have affected her mediumship. Public interest in her writing also faded, and in December 1937, Pearl Curran died of pneumonia, leaving Patience silent once more.

The real question of this story is, who was Pearl Curran speaking with? Was it the spirit of a woman named Patience Worth, was it some discarnate entity lying about its identity, or was Pearl simply tapping into her own unconscious mind? It is this lack of certainty in knowing with whom a person is really communicating that causes investigators and psychics alike to view the Ouija board as both controversial and dangerous.

AUTOMATIC WRITING

This form of writing occurs when a medium enters into an altered state of consciousness and allows a spirit or other entity to gain control of his or her hand muscles in order to write messages. The medium holding the pen is often not aware of what is being written and the message may even appear in a handwriting style unlike that of the writer. In some cases, these messages may even be written in a language unfamiliar to the medium. Still, many skeptics claim that what is being written is nothing more than the thoughts of a person's subconscious mind bubbling to the surface and forming a split personality. In fact, modern psychologists sometimes use automatic writing as a therapeutic tool for patients suffering from multiple personality disorder.

The most celebrated case of automatic writing occurred not at the séance table, but in the Bristol architectural office of Frederick Bligh Bond early in the twentieth century. Bond had recently been placed in charge of excavations at Glastonbury Abbey, thought to be one of the first Christian churches in England. Legend claimed that it was founded by Saint Patrick himself and even held the remains of the fabled King Arthur. Legends aside, it was known for certain to have been a holy place of great prestige until Henry VIII destroyed it in the sixteenth century. Envious of its lands and wealth, Henry had wasted no time in acquiring the site while driving the Catholic Church out of England.

On November 7, 1907, Bond and an associate named John Allen Bartlett sat down with pen and paper for their first psychic experiment with automatic writing. Almost immediately they were amazed as Bartlett drew a map of a chapel no one knew existed and signed it Gulielmus Monachus—William the Monk. Over the remainder of the dig, Bond received many similar messages revealing the locations of structures unknown to himself or anyone else still alive. These were written at first in a medieval Latin script and then in archaic English by a host of spirit monks calling themselves "the watchers from the other side."

Bond's success seemed assured until he made the mistake in 1917 of telling the church committee which sponsored the dig that his discoveries rested upon information gathered from the spirit world. Initially only frustrated with Bond's claims, they soon became enraged when in 1918 he published his account in a book entitled *Gate of Remembrance*. In retaliation, the church gradually stripped Bond of his responsibilities until 1921, when he was completely squeezed out. To this day, the church continues to ban his book from the Glastonbury Abbey bookstore.

There are those who claim that these spirit writings could have come from less unusual sources. After all, both Bond and Bartlett were well-versed in medieval history, languages, and architecture. In addition, many of the writings were either too vague to understand or just plain wrong. Bond himself, however, discredited the notion that he was really communicating with the spirits of long-dead monks. Rather, he believed there exists a pool of human knowledge and experience collected through time. If a person were sensitive enough, he or she could draw from this source and tune in to all of mankind's secrets.

DIRECT WRITING

Although similar to automatic writing, this form of communication is directly attributed to a spiritual agent and does not require the presence of a medium's body for action. In its heyday, it proved a quick and easy method compared to others being used by mediums at the time. During a séance, a medium had only to place a piece of paper and a writing instrument into a sealed envelope or box. Then, with his or her hands atop it, he or she would call out to the spirits, commanding that they communicate. Usually, after a few minutes of silence to add to the effect, the medium would begin to convulse, and all about the room the feverish sounds of scribbling could be heard. After a few more theatrics, he or she would remove the paper from the container to reveal an answer written in the spirit's own hand. Such messages have also appeared on photographic plates and plaster walls, scratched upon human skin, and typed out via typewriters.

One of the most famous direct writing mediums of the nineteenth century was Dr. Henry Slade (the title "Dr." he adopted for himself). His method of direct writing involved using a small chalkboard similar to those used by schoolchildren during his day. The board was the type that could be folded onto itself like a book and then fastened shut. He placed this with a piece of chalk under a table, one end of which he held while the other end was held by one of the sitters. After a few spooky dramatics, he pulled the board out from under the table to reveal a message written by the hand of some spirit. This method was a delight with sitters and was popularly termed "slate-writing." Slade became an instant success and traveled the world at the request of several different European nobles. Some of his new converts were eminent men of science whom he won over with his ability to materialize ghostly hands that miraculously wrote messages upon sealed tablets.

Yet for Henry Slade, disaster always seemed to follow him. In London in 1876, he was tried and found guilty of taking money under false pretenses. Under appeal, the verdict was thrown out for technical matters and Slade hastily left the country. Then in America in 1885, he was charged with fraud after giving a séance for the Seybert Commission in Philadelphia. One year later, in Weston, West Virginia, he was charged with deceiving the public. In addition, several investigators published books documenting the fraudulent practices that they encountered during Slade's séances. Given this continual stream of bad publicity, his career deteriorated quickly and Henry Slade died in a Michigan sanatorium in 1905. His legacy of slate-writing became a popular trick among fraudulent mediums, and trick slates could be ordered in a wide range of models through the mail.

Ectoplasm

Ectoplasm is a theoretical substance believed to be exuded by the medium's body during a séance that allowed spirits to materialize. The word "ectoplasm" is comprised of two Greek words, *ektos* and *plasma*, meaning "exteriorized substance." This term was first used by French physiologist Charles Richet in 1894 to explain a third arm or *pseudopod* that emanated from the medium Eusapia Palladino during séances. Reports of witnessed ectoplasm varied greatly from case to case, and each medium seemed to have his or her own signature form. Some ectoplasm was said to be hot to the touch, have weight, and move in relation to the medium's body, while others claim it was cold, rubbery, and dough-like. Its reported shapes ran the spectrum from amorphous clouds to thin, waving tentacles or wide, membrane-like netting. It could appear to be a solid, a liquid, or a gas, was often milky-white in color, and sometimes smelled of ozone.

Ectoplasm was thought to be able to emanate from any orifice of the medium's body, no matter how small or private. This could include the mouth, ears, eyes, nose, navel, nipples, or vagina, depending on the medium. Spiritualists of the early twentieth century believed that spirits relied upon this substance as a means to materialize, produce raps, tilt tables, and produce other phenomena. The energy in ectoplasm was thought to give physical consistency to spiritual structures, which allowed spirits to contact and interact with beings on this plane of existence.

Unfortunately, ectoplasm proved impossible to study because mediums claimed that it would disappear if exposed to light and that it could only be viewed in the darkness of the séance room, surrounded by those who believed. This, of course, made laboratory testing impossible and caused many "unbelievers" to view the ectoplasmic phenomenon as nothing more than a cheap magic trick. Of the evidence that did survive, close examination showed the "ectoplasm" to be nothing more than chewed paper, gauze, fabric, or animal tissue that the medium regurgitated during the séance.

One medium of the 1920s, Mina Crandon, became famous for producing ectoplasm during her sittings. At the height of the séance, she was even able to produce a tiny ectoplasmic hand from her navel, which waved about in the darkness. Her career ended when Harvard biologists were able to examine the tiny hand and found it to be nothing more than a carved piece of animal liver.

Apports and Asports

When an object appears as if formed from thin air or as though it has passed through solid matter, it is called an *apport*, from the French word *apporter*, meaning "to bring." This phenomenon certainly added a bit of color to the average séance and mediums wasted no time in materializing a wide assortment of objects. These appeared in every imaginable size and shape, and included flowers, perfumes, live animals, and even rare gems. Some of these did more than just appear; some even took off and flew about the room. Imagine the shock sitters would receive when, in the darkness of the séance room, gems fell into their lap or they were struck in the head by a baby shark.

The reverse of this process is known as an *asport*, and occurs when an object is made to disappear. Harry Houdini wrote of one of D. D. Home's more infamous asports in his book A *Magician Among Spirits*. It seems that Home had a great fondness for jewels and during one séance he asported an emerald necklace belonging to a member of the Russian court. The noble was thoroughly entertained—that is, until the spirits refused to give the necklace back. The police were then called in and upon searching Home, the jewels were discovered in his pocket. Home, of course, claimed the spirits were simply playing a bad joke on him, but the inspector did not share the spirits' sense of humor and warned Home that Russia was no longer a healthy place for him. Home immediately left the country.

There are three basic explanations for how these two phenomena occur. The first and easiest explanation is that they are faked. Numerous occasions have been documented where mediums were caught hiding objects on their person or about the room before the séance. It would then require little more than a bit of sleight of hand to make objects suddenly appear as if from thin air. The second is a theory suggested by German psychical researcher Johann Zollner. His belief was that either a spirit or the medium unconsciously lifted the object into a dimension above our own. Once there, it could be brought to its desired spot and then reintegrated back into our three-dimensional space. The final theory proposes that matter can be disintegrated, and then the molecular elements moved to a destination where they are put back together again. If this theory were true, then according to the laws of energy transmutation, objects that were apported would produce heat. Interestingly enough, researchers studying poltergeist disturbances found that objects that were moved about or apported by poltergeists often seemed hot to the touch afterward.

SPIRIT VOICES

Despite all the table shaking, ghostly knocking, and objects appearing and disappearing at will, what sitters wanted most at the séance table was to hear the spirits speak. At first, mediums used a technique known as direct voice phenomenon (DVP), which involved the spirit speaking directly through the medium's vocal apparatus. Often this occurred at a point in space very near to where the medium was seated, and with the aid of a trumpet that floated about the room. Allegedly, the trumpet acted as both a condenser of psychic energy and an amplifier of the spirit's voice.

The spirits that chose to speak during these sessions were a wide mix of colorful characters ranging from Indian chiefs to pirate captains. After all, the more exotic the spirit, the more entertaining the séance, and who wanted to attend a séance that wasn't exciting? On many occasions, particular spirits would attach themselves to a medium and act as a spirit guide between the land of the living and that of the dead. These were known as "controls" and at times gained more fame than the mediums they served. One such spirit control called itself John King, and first made an appearance in a séance conducted by the Davenport brothers, William and Ira, in 1850. John claimed that his real name was Henry Owen Morgan, an English pirate who terrorized Jamaica in the 1600s. King, however, could never sit still for very long and made his rounds among various famous mediums of the time. Brash and boastful, he claimed responsibility for many strange feats, from apporting a three-hundred-pound

medium named Mrs. Angus Guppy during a séance to in-
venting the spirit trumpet used in DVP.

By the mid-1900s, the nature of the séance began to change
as the public demanded more credible methods from mediums. Many of the more easily faked phenomena that captivated earlier sitters were no longer practiced and, by the
1970s, DVP had evolved into a new form of communication
known as channeling. The medium began by placing himself
into a trance or altered state of consciousness. In this state,
the spirit could enter the body of the medium and physically
use him to speak through. During channeling, the medium's
mannerisms, inflections, and speech changed drastically as
the spirit's personality took over. Cases have been recorded
describing mediums that suddenly began to speak fluently in
a language foreign to them.

Some skeptics have cited the unconscious mind of the
medium as the true source of these spirit communications.
In the absence of the conscious mind during altered states,
repressed or forgotten information floods to the surface,
forming a personality of its own in a process known as cryp-
tomnesia. An early example of this occurred in 1874 with
the medium William Stanton Moses, who communicated
with the spirits of two brothers who had recently died in
India. Upon investigation, it was discovered that one week
prior to the séance, their obituary had appeared in the newspaper. This was of some importance because Moses's communications with the two spirits contained nothing that
wasn't already printed in the newspaper. When the spirits
were pressed for further information, they were unable to

provide any. Researchers concluded that Moses had seen the obituary, forgotten it, and then resurfaced the memory during the séance. Not only did the memory float back to the surface but, interestingly enough, it formed itself into the personalities of the two recently departed spirits.

———•———

Although the means by which we approach the subject has changed over time, the question is still the same: Can the spirits of the dead return? Our ancestors certainly thought so and devised a number of methods both simple and complex to prove their existence. Some of those described in this chapter are still used by professional mediums as well as the average person looking for some good, scary fun. Calling a 1-900 number has largely replaced sitting in a dark séance room, but the appeal that the spirits hold has yet to diminish.

Chapter 5

THINGS THAT GO BUMP IN THE NIGHT: APPARITIONS

. . . *out of the stillness, little, scarcely perceptible noises began to emphasize themselves. The ticking of the clock began to bring itself into notice. Old beams began to crack mysteriously. The stairs creaked faintly. Evidently spirits were abroad.*

— MARK TWAIN, *The Adventures of Tom Sawyer*

*E*ver wake from a dream with the sensation that some-one or something has just roused you from sleep? Then, as you lay there rubbing your eyes, the room suddenly grows cold, sending the hair on your arms and neck to prickle into tiny goose bumps. From somewhere in the house a floorboard creaks, first one and then another, until the noises sound like soft footsteps pacing outside your bedroom door. Your heart beats faster as you strain your ears in the darkness. Getting out of bed, you move toward the door. Is it just your imagination or is someone or something in the house with you? Should you crawl back under the warm, safe covers of your bed, or do you turn the handle of the door? Fear wells up in your tightening chest as you grasp the handle and, holding your breath, you swing open the door. But there's nothing there! The footsteps have stopped and the hall is empty of all but a little moonlight streaming in from the window. You are alone. In the morning, the room is warm again and bathed in sunlight. You laugh at the fact that you let your imagination scare you with a few silly sounds. After all, it was just your imagination, right?

If you have ever experienced a moment like this, either your imagination gave you a really good scare or you've experienced what in the field of the paranormal is known as an apparition. Originally derived from the Latin term *apparere*, meaning "to appear," the term today is used to cover a wide range of unexplained phenomena. For the purposes of this discussion, we will define an apparition as the supernatural appearance of a dead person or animal, an object, or even a living person who is not physically present. It would seem very easy to jump to the conclusion that apparitions are ghosts; however, there is a very important distinction between the two. A ghost is considered the actual spirit of a once-living person returned from the dead, while an apparition is a hallucination in one form or another. Therefore, to confuse you even further, an apparition may appear as a ghost but a ghost is not an apparition.

Those encountering apparitions report a bewildering array of phenomena that differs in so many regards that finding patterns in their appearance and behavior can be difficult. For instance, apparitions may at times appear with what seems a real and definable form that can be (and has been) mistaken for everyday objects and people. In these cases, apparitions have been witnessed casting shadows on the ground and reflections in mirrors, as well as moving objects and interacting with others to the point of even allowing themselves to be touched. At the other end of the scale, some appear as nothing more than cloudy or transparent figures floating through walls or moving along passageways that no longer exist, oblivious to anyone around them. Finally, some have been known to appear to a particular individual and yet go unnoticed by anyone else present, while on other occasions apparitions have startled entire crowds of onlookers.

To better understand exactly what these manifestations were, a group of Cambridge University scholars began meeting in London in 1882, as the Society for Psychical Research (SPR). Their aim was to study not only apparition manifestations, but also such phenomena as extrasensory perception, poltergeist activity, and the rising Spiritualist movement. Over time, the society attracted many famous men of science and letters like Sir Oliver Lodge, Sigmund Freud, Carl Jung, and the inventor of the fictional super-sleuth Sherlock Holmes, Sir Arthur Conan Doyle.

Their first task was to conduct a massive survey to collect and record the experiences of people who had witnessed apparition manifestations. To their surprise, the survey caused case after case to pour in, reported by people from every walk of life. Even after separating cases that did not stand up to scrutiny, there still remained 701 cases worthy of attention, which they published in an 1886 book entitled *Phantasms of the Living*. This work, along with Henry Sidgwick's *Census of Hallucinations*, is still being referred to by researchers today. What the SPR learned from this study was not only that many different types of people claimed to have witnessed apparitions, but that because of the vast differences from one experience to another, classifying and understanding the phenomena would be a daunting task. Even in light of today's technological advances, scientists involved in study of the paranormal differ on how best to approach the subject.

In this book, in an attempt to keep an already confusing topic as simple as possible, we will divide them into apparitions of the living, the dead, and the non-human.

Apparitions of the Living

One common misconception is that apparitions resemble some long-dead specter roaming a moonlit moor, accompanied by a creepy movie soundtrack. Surprisingly enough, early studies such as those by the SPR revealed that two-thirds of all sightings involved apparitions of people that were still alive at the time of the sighting. Throughout history these sightings have been known to many cultures and have been given names such as double, doppelganger, and wraith. In most cases, they seem so real that they've been mistaken for the flesh and blood counterpart they resemble.

The writer Mark Twain was fond of telling a story concerning a large reception that he was attending one evening. Through the crowd of guests, he spied a woman he knew and liked very much. Thinking to say hello, he made his way through the sea of faces to the spot where she had stood, only to find her gone. Some time later, upon meeting her again, he was perplexed to discover that she had not been at the reception at all. Instead, she was still on the train en route to the party and wearing the same gown that Twain had observed her double wearing. This type of manifestation is known as an "arrival apparition," and occurs when a person is thinking of taking a trip somewhere or is eagerly expected to arrive at a particular location. The desire on either the part of the traveler or the one expecting him seems to create the double, which acts, looks, and dresses identically to the one making the journey. In most cases, however, the double disappears before the person arrives, and there are few reports of a person running into his own double.

The Norwegians have a similar apparition that they call a *vardoger* or "forerunner," which consists of auditory manifestations such as the sounds a person would make coming home before he or she actually arrived. For instance, the sound of a person's footsteps approaching, knocking at the door, or even the sound of keys being inserted into the door's lock. When the person answers the door, expecting to greet his guest, he finds no one there. But soon after, the guest can be expected to arrive, preceded by the very same sounds his *vardoger* made before him.

One of the most astonishing cases of an arrival apparition involved an American importer named Erikson Gorique. For years, Gorique had wanted to travel to Norway, but for one reason or another had to postpone the trip. In 1955, an opportunity arose for him to travel to the city of Oslo to purchase glassware and china, and Gorique jumped at the chance. Without making any prior plans, he made his way to the city and inquired as to which hotel was the best. Before long, he was directed to a desirable hotel and, upon entering the lobby, was greeted warmly by the clerk on duty, who welcomed him back again. Of course, Gorique thought that there must have been some kind of mistake and informed the clerk that this was his first trip to Norway, never before having set foot in the hotel or even the city, for that matter. Nonetheless the clerk was adamant, claiming that

Gorique had stayed at the hotel a number of times and that he even recognized Gorique's unusual last name. Not only that, but three months prior, during what the clerk claimed was Gorique's most recent trip, he said Gorique had made reservations to return to the hotel on that very day. Amazed at the occurrence, Gorique checked in and went to meet with the local wholesale dealer to purchase china and glassware. Here, too, the dealer greeted him as if he were well known and stated that he was only too happy to conclude the business transaction that he said Gorique had initiated three months earlier. When Gorique, with great confusion, related the incidents of his trip thus far, the dealer only smiled and told him that it must have been his double and that in Norway "such things are not uncommon."

Another type of apparition involves the unusual claim that certain individuals possess the ability to intentionally produce a double of their own. This "experimental apparition," as it's called, occurs when a person concentrates on projecting his image to someone or someplace else. While doing this, the projector is not aware of whether or not the image is being successfully duplicated. In this regard, the process should not be mistaken for a very similar one known as "astral projection," in which the projector enters an alternate state of consciousness, is fully aware of his astral double, and maintains complete control over it.

S. H. Beard was a man with an obvious sense of humor, and one night he decided to project an image of himself to his fiancée, Miss L. S. Verity. He began the experiment by lying down in his bedroom and concentrating on the image of his fiancée. Several miles away, Miss Verity was preparing for bed in a room that she shared with her eleven-year-old sister. At the time, she was not aware of Beard's intentions, and upon turning round from the mirror she watched Beard's double materialize before her. Her reaction to the event was a normal one—she immediately screamed. This in turn woke her sister, who recognized the double as Beard's and also screamed. With all the screaming, Beard's double vanished as quickly as it came. During a social visit some days later, the two girls related to Beard what they had witnessed that night. They made him swear that if he had any more intentions of projecting his image, he was to understand that "a proper young lady's room" was no place for a man—real or not.

English bedrooms are not the only place apparitions have been projected. Halfway around the world in the snow-peaked mountains of Tibet there is a tradition concerning apparitions known as *tulpas*. It is believed that a Buddhist monk, while in a perfect state of concentration, may produce an apparition that can resemble anything he chooses, including animals, demons, gods, buildings, or even an image of himself. Once created, the *tulpas* look, feel, and act like the object that they duplicate, and many stories are told in the Buddhist traditions of wily Lamas deceiving others with their *tulpas*. It is said that in the early 1900s, when the ruling Lama was forced to flee his country into exile, he left behind a *tulpa* of himself on the throne to deceive everyone. Once he reached the relative safety of the border, the *tulpa* vanished before a stunned crowd of onlookers.

To test these claims, French explorer and spiritualist Al-exandra David-Néel attempted to produce one of her own during her travels in the Himalayas in the 1920s. She began by placing herself in a *tsams*, or solitude hut, and after performing the long, complicated rites necessary, was able to produce the image of a fat, jolly monk. She brought this apparition along on a journey with her and recorded that in every way it acted like a real traveler. At first it was only visible to her, but soon others in the party began to see the monk and mistake it for one of their group. As time went on, however, the apparition seemed to develop a personality of its own. It grew leaner, sly, and mocking, until David-Néel was no longer able to control it. When she could stand the troublesome monk no longer, she began the rites to dissolve it. These took six months of intense mental concentration, against which the monk fought bitterly before being forced to vanish for good. David-Néel spent many years in Tibet studying Buddhism and Tibetan occultism and was the first European woman to enter the Forbidden City of Lhasa, for which she became world famous in 1924.

Since the late 1800s, when groups such as the SPR began to study this phenomenon, it was noticed that most cases fell into a category known as "crisis apparitions." This type of apparition is projected by people under great personal stress or trauma, as in times of illness or at the moment of their death. The created doubles tend to appear to someone that they have a close emotional tie with, like a family member or longtime friend. In most cases, they seem driven to convey their distress to the witness and inform him or her of their condition by drawing attention to their wounds or even replaying their tragedy.

One classic example often retold by writers of the paranormal is that of a young boy named G. F. Russell Colt, who was living with his family in Edinburgh, Scotland. On the night of September 8, 1855, Russell awoke to find the figure of his older brother Oliver kneeling at the foot of his bed, covered in a glowing mist. Oliver was a lieutenant in the 7th Royal Fusiliers, fighting in the Crimean War at the time. Not believing his own eyes, Russell closed them and tried to tell himself that it was just a trick of the moonlight shining in through his window. Yet when he opened them again, he found the image of his brother still there, staring back at him sadly. This was too much for the young boy, who promptly jumped out of bed and fled the room. In doing so, he looked back on the glowing figure and noticed that it had a terrible wound on its right temple, from which blood poured out. The next day, Russell told his father what he had seen and was ordered never to repeat such "nonsense" to anyone. As far as the father was concerned, the boy had merely had a bad dream and shouldn't worry the rest of the family with his wild tales. Several weeks later, however, the family received a chilling letter informing them that their son Oliver had died storming the Turkish fortifications at Sebastopol. A bullet had struck him in the right temple on September 8, 1855, the very night he appeared to his younger brother.

Was this nothing more than a young boy letting his imagination run wild, as his father thought, or could Oliver, as he lay dying on some distant battlefield, have been thinking of his younger brother and projecting an image of himself to warn Russell of his passing? The boy's detailed account of his brother's death and the location of his wound is an example of "veridical knowledge" and occurs when specific information is conveyed by the apparition to the recipient—information that could not have been known by the recipient at the time and which, upon later verification, proves to be true. Veridical information often provides credibility to cases involving crisis apparitions.

Death, however, is not the only circumstance known to produce crisis apparitions, and it is thought that the strain of bodily injury or illness may have the same effect. For instance, there was a letter published by the SPR involving a woman known as Mrs. Ashley of Bristol. One sunny afternoon, Mrs. Ashley was busy in the kitchen at the back of the house when she distinctly heard her son calling her name. Thinking that he had returned home from working at the plant several miles away, she noted the time to be 3:30 p.m. She called back a greeting, but got no reply and so began searching the house for him. When she could not find him, she questioned Miss Dodd, with whom she shared the house, but she had heard nothing. A little confused, she dismissed the affair and went back to her chores until several hours later when a knocking at the door interrupted her. Upon answering the door, she was handed a letter that informed her that at exactly 3:30 p.m. that day, her son's arm was horribly crushed in an accident at work and he was rushed to a nearby hospital. The plant manager verified the time of the accident for researchers, and Mrs. Ashley reported that there was no mistaking the fact that she had heard her son's voice call out to her at that time.

As early researchers such as the SPR looked at these and other cases, they developed the theory that apparitions were nothing more than telepathic projections. In some instances, they believed, both the living and the dead have the ability to project a telepathic impulse to someone and provide a sort of rough sketch of their personality. Once this image was received, the person's senses would flesh out the rest and form an image of the apparition. At times when numerous individuals saw a phantom simultaneously, researchers proposed that a type of "telepathic infection" occurred, where one person received the telepathic impulse and then projected that image to the minds of those around him or her. By this means, everyone in a room could see the same hallucination.

Unfortunately, theories of telepathy were just not able to explain manifestations adequately and many questions remained (and remain) unanswered. Early in the twentieth century, researchers were in dire need to cast the phenomenon in terms that legitimized it as a science. To do otherwise ran the risk of dooming the fledgling field of parapsychology back to the superstition of Spiritualism from which it sprang. To alleviate some of the inconsistencies in the telepathy theory, psychical researcher Frederic Myers pushed forward the concept of a "phantasogenetic centre." This supposedly occurred when the personality of the projector was so powerful that it created a space around the witness in which it could shape the environment to its will.

The problem with the theories of Myers and his contemporaries is that although they help explain apparitions of the living to some degree, they often fall short when applied to other types of apparitions. Stretched to the point of breaking, telepathy theories have fallen out of favor over the years to be replaced by more flexible models.

APPARITIONS OF THE DEAD

These types of apparitions encompass those cases in which the image that appears to witnesses resembles that of a person who is no longer living. In today's terminology, these figures are referred to as "postmortem apparitions" and can be divided between those that are transient and those that are continual. Transient apparitions are by far the more common of the two and are given the name because they appear only for a brief time, after which they are not seen again. For example, in one case, a woman living in California stepped out of the house to watch her husband work on a motorcycle he had just purchased when she noticed a young man standing over his shoulder, watching the repairs with great interest. When she called out to her husband, the young man behind him looked up at her and vanished into thin air. To her surprise, her husband claimed that he was alone the entire time and was not aware of anyone behind him. Later, the couple learned that the previous owner of the motorcycle had died in an accident while driving it and that he matched the description of the apparition the woman had seen. Like apparitions of the living, postmortem apparitions that are transient appear to be ordinary living people.

It isn't until the apparition has disappeared, or much later, that witnesses realize that what they had seen was no living person, but a phantom.

Did the apparition of the young man return to warn the present owner of his death by the very motorcycle being repaired, or was he simply returning to see how his old bike was holding up? Postmortem apparitions are often attached in some way to a place or object that the person cherished in life. Their image returns to the things they loved, the things they were linked to in their former existence. In Docia Williams's book *Best Tales of Texas Ghosts*, she relates a story that further demonstrates the connection between the apparition and an object, or in this case, a place. One of the ushers at the mission of San Jose de San Miguel de Aguayo, in San Antonio, Texas, was approached one sunny afternoon by an elderly woman. She told him that her name was Mrs. Huizar and she wanted to know what time the mass started. He asked her to wait there while he ran into the church to get the bulletin that listed the times, but when he returned she was gone. Upon mentioning this to another church worker who claimed to know the woman, he was told it couldn't have been her. She had died more than fifty years prior.

In the above examples, the returning apparitions were a stranger to the witnesses and, although fully capable of interaction, seemed more intent on going about their own business. Those that return to someone they are familiar with, however, usually do so for the purpose of communicating with them. For instance, F. G. was a commercial traveler staying the night in a hotel in St. Joseph, Missouri.

He was working late, filling out mountains of paperwork and smoking, when he felt someone next to him. Turning around, he saw the apparition of his sister who had died nine years before of cholera. She immediately vanished, but before she did he noticed an angry red scar down the length of her right cheek. When he returned home and told his mother what he had witnessed, she nearly fainted and broke down into tears. During the preparation of his sister's body for burial, she had accidentally scratched the girl's face with her ring and tried to cover it up with makeup. She had told no one what happened.

Sometimes a postmortem apparition will continue to manifest over a period of time in a specific location, forming what is traditionally considered a "haunting." This may continue for years or even centuries, becoming mixed with the stuff of legends and bedtime stories. In some cases, the apparition fluctuates between periods of activity and dormancy, sometimes skipping entire generations when not active, only to resurface again much later. When the activity does begin anew, usually some change in the apparition's environment has triggered the haunting again. There are many tales of old houses that slept quietly until some new, unsuspecting family moved in and began renovations. This helps to illustrate the fact that what separates a haunting from other manifestations is that it is bound to some particular geographic location. The word "haunt" itself comes from the same root as the word "home," which is no mere coincidence as postmortem apparitions often return to the place they knew best in life, their home.

Raynham Hall is located just outside Norfolk, England, and was built in the 1600s in the grand style of English manors as the family seat of the Marquises of Townshend. This was about all Captain Provand and Indra Shira knew in 1936 when they arrived to photograph the ancient manor for *Country Life* magazine. As they set up their bulky plate camera and tripod, Shira pointed to a grand staircase that rose to the floors above and, while shouting to Provand, he took a picture. Provand saw nothing unusual at the time, but upon developing the plate there was no mistaking that it had captured a wispy, phantomlike figure of a woman in a long white dress and veil descending the staircase. The photograph was published in *Country Life*, and has since been scrutinized by many experts, although none have been able to prove it a fake.

The lady of Raynham Hall, as she became known, had been roaming the corridors of the dusty old manor for many years before Provand and Shira photographed her, and had by this time become a permanent fixture in the Townshend family's history. Legend recounts that the figure is that of the second wife of the Marquis Charles Townshend, Lady Dorothy Walpole Townshend. When the lord discovered that, before their marriage, she had been the mistress of Lord Wharton, he had her locked away in Raynham Hall, where she died in 1726. The exact cause of death is unknown. It may have been due to smallpox, a fall down the grand staircase, or in the more romantic versions, a broken heart.

Her first recorded appearance was during the Christmas season of 1835, when a guest of the house, a Colonel Loftus, was retiring to his room for the night and literally ran into, or through, the apparition gliding down the corridor. Loftus later sketched what he saw, and then had it painted and hung in one of the manor's rooms. The apparition, he claimed, had been wearing a brown satin dress from an older period and had a glowing face with no eyes. Legend has it that, although the painting appears harmless in the daylight, when viewed at night by candlelight it takes on a sinister, skeletal aspect.

Years later Lady Townshend was encountered again, this time by another guest who was also a military man. Captain Frederick Marryat had listened to his hosts tell stories of the phantom all evening, and then in the true spirit of adventure, announced that he would spend the night in the room that was believed to have belonged to her in life. That night, he and two companions lay in wait in the corridor outside the room when the figure of a woman with a glowing lantern approached them. As she passed where they had concealed themselves, she turned and smiled diabolically. In his panic, the captain fired his pistol point-blank into the phantom as it vanished. The next morning, the family gathered at the scene and found the bullet lodged in the wall where it had passed through the figure. From that time on, Lady Townshend appeared only infrequently, either on the staircase or in one of the corridors, until her last appearance, for the photographers of *Country Life*. She has not been seen since.

Although the legend of the lady of Raynham Hall embodies many of the stereotypical elements of a haunting, apparitions have a history of appearing in some of the most unlikely places, including a famous luxury liner. When the *Queen Mary* left port in 1934, she was one of the largest ships in the world and made transatlantic voyages from England to New York until the beginning of World War II. Once a floating palace for the rich and famous, she was painted a camouflage gray and enlisted into the Royal Navy as a troop carrier. The soldiers that she shuttled to the war front came to call her "the Grey Ghost," and Hitler himself offered any U-boat commander that sank her a $250,000 reward and an Iron Cross. Yet no matter how adept the *Queen Mary* may have been at dodging German torpedoes, she wasn't able to avoid tragedy and, while performing maneuvers one day, she sliced into the hull of the British cruiser H.M.S. *Curacao*, sending the smaller ship to the bottom along with more than three hundred British soldiers.

After the war, she returned to her role as cruise ship until ending her service in 1967, when she became a permanently moored hotel in Long Beach, California. Yet some believe that for the *Queen Mary* and her guests, there is no escaping the past, and during the ship's time as a hotel many strange occurrences have taken place within her decks. Both visitors and staff have reported seeing the apparitions of deceased crewmembers and passengers from long ago still wandering the ship. One of the most frequently appearing is that of a bearded man in blue coveralls walking the length of what is known as "shaft alley," where in 1966 a young fireman named John Reeder was crushed to death in a watertight door during a drill. The clothing in which the apparition is seen matches what Reeder was wearing that fateful day.

In addition, odd sounds sometimes echo through the hallways at night—sounds of splashing water from the empty first class pool or a baby's cry from the third class children's playroom. Lights come on by themselves and guests have complained about the sound of heavy breathing or people tugging at their blankets when they were alone in their room. Reports such as these gave the ship an even greater reputation than it had in all its days at sea, and it has been made something of a tourist attraction today by those hoping to catch a glimpse of the past. On one occasion, a television crew left an audio recorder on overnight in the exact spot where the *Queen Mary* collided with the H.M.S. *Curacao*. When the crew played back the tape the next day, they were astonished to hear screams and the sounds of banging.

Some researchers view hauntings as the residual playback of accumulated impressions from the past. They theorize that, over time, a house or other structure can act as a psychic storehouse for the emotions of its past occupants. Under the right conditions, a person can enter such a room and feel strong emotions or experience phantoms from the past, played back much the way a record produces music when the needle touches its surface. In addition to the human factor, hauntings may also be triggered by other elements such as weather conditions or a specific time of the day.

Oftentimes, a haunted location has been the scene of a tragedy. Incidents involving strong emotions such as sorrow, fear, or hatred create deep impressions in the environment that can bind an apparition to a site. These negative emotions act as a sort of prison for the apparition, doomed to reenacting its tragedy over and over again. Even though Raynham Hall and the *Queen Mary* differ greatly in matters such as location and type of manifestations, what they do have in common is that they were both the scenes of powerful emotional tragedies. In one case, heartbreak, imprisonment, and death (possibly murder), and in the other, accidents that caused the loss of hundreds of lives. Like other types of hauntings, those that center on tragedies manifest at times when there is a link of some sort between the past and the present, and may even occur on the anniversary of the tragedy.

The Tower of London is one of the bloodiest places ever built by man and has served as both a prison and a place of execution for countless victims who fell before the axe. One of these unfortunates was Margaret Pole, the Countess of Salisbury, who appears on the anniversary of her death replaying the ghastly scene for anyone who might be present. Her botched execution occurred in 1541, when, after three unsuccessful swings with the axe, the countess broke free from her captors and ran about the walled yard, screaming hysterically for help. Subdued by guards, she was dragged back to the block, fighting all the way, where she received a fourth blow that cut only halfway through her neck and left her choking on her own blood. Finally, a fifth blow ended the torture, and since then more than one stunned guardsman has reported that, on the anniversary of her death, her apparition is seen running about the yard as if being pursued while her ghostly screams fill the air.

NON-HUMAN APPARITIONS

To assume that all apparitions are of human agents is to make a rather (pardon me for the pun) grave mistake. The history of apparitions is filled with all manner of images, from the spectral black dogs of the English coast to phantom trains that speed along deserted tracks under a full moon. These non-human apparitions, as we classify them, differ little from their human counterparts. Thus a drowning horse could project an image of itself to its owner much like a human crisis apparition, or a room could continue to be haunted with the faint sounds of piano music long after any instrument was kept there. Whatever the ultimate cause of the phenomenon, it is obvious that humans do not have a monopoly on the apparitional market.

The idea that animals have appeared as apparitions can be traced back through some of man's earliest literature and legends. Our ancestors believed that if a person could return from the dead, then certainly an animal could also. These phantom creatures were greatly feared and in many legends were assigned the role of death omens. None, however, were more terrifying than the Black Shuck of the British Isles. Folklore has it that a large, coal-black dog, savage in appearance with burning red eyes, haunted the coasts and deserted countryside at night. To spy one meant certain doom and ensured a person that he would meet his death within the year. The origin of this belief has been lost in the mists of time, but some claim that it was a convenient way for smugglers to keep nosy townsfolk away from the coasts at night while they were plying their illegal trade. Regardless of its source, the fact remains that images of ghostly animals have haunted man as powerfully as any other.

Of all the specters that seem trapped within the Tower of London's walls, one story stands out from the rest. Unlike some others, however, this recurring apparition is not of a bungling nobleman who managed to lose his head; this is the story of a bear. The apparition made its first appearance on a cold October night in 1817. A sentry making his rounds outside Martin Tower, part of the Tower of London complex, watched with amazement as vapor poured through a narrow gap between a closed door and the seal. This was no ordinary mist, however, as it began to form into the shape of a bear. The guard, with a certainly understandable sense of fear, lunged at the beast with his bayonet, which passed through the figure and lodged in the wooden door behind it. The story continues with the guardsman fainting with fright and expiring a short time later. Although this last bit seems nothing short of poetic fancy, the incident embodies many elements found in more traditional human hauntings. Regardless of its embellishments, the tale is not devoid of particular facts. According to historical records, part of the Tower was once used as a royal menagerie and held bear baiting sessions that pitted chained bears against vicious hounds in a contest to the death.

For centuries, men and women who argued for the existence of a soul or some form of survival after bodily death have drawn from the vast pool of apparition manifestations as proof of its existence. At first, attention was focused on postmortem apparitions of humans as evidence of this, but more recently investigators have turned increasingly to the study of animal apparitions as well. After all, we are not too far removed from our animal cousins, and if we possess this ability, why not them also? Nonetheless, when sifting through the mountains of cases concerning apparitions, we run into a real stumbling block. Numerous reports relate to apparitions that are neither human, nor animal, nor were they ever alive to begin with.

The least frequent type of reported apparition manifestation is of inanimate objects ranging from phantom vehicles such as trains, cars, or even planes to large structures like a house. Although these never existed as living beings, in many instances those that appear are seemingly tied to humanity and tragedy all the same. When President Abraham Lincoln was assassinated at the close of the War between the States by a Southern sympathizer, plans were made to transfer his body from the nation's capitol to his home in Springfield, Illinois, for its final rest. For this purpose, a special train was outfitted to carry his body from Washington to Illinois, stopping at every major city along the way so that the immense crowds that gathered could pay their respects. The trip took about two weeks, but some claim it continues still. In April, on the anniversary of Lincoln's death, a phantom train has been reported near Urbana and Piqua, Illinois, roaring along the tracks that the funeral car once used. Stories tell that the train races by at night, draped in black and playing a funeral dirge. The last car is said to be a flat car that bears the president's coffin, still waiting to make its way home. The *Albany Evening Times* even wrote once of its passing:

It passes noiselessly. If it is moonlight, clouds come over the moon as the phantom train goes by. After the pilot engine passes, the funeral's train itself with flags and streamers rushes past. The track seems covered with black carpet, and the coffin is seen in the center of the car. . . .

If a real train were passing its noise would be hushed as if the phantom train rode over it. Clocks and watches always stop as the phantom train goes by and when looked at are five to eight minutes behind.

There are many stories of this sort of phenomenon, equally as famous, such as the cursed ship, the *Flying Dutchman*, seen by sailors plying the dark, stormy seas hundreds of years after it sank to the bottom of Davy Jones's locker with all hands still aboard. Yet there are others that are not as popular and leave no discernable clue as to their origin, forever remaining an enigma to be chased by men on dark nights when the moon and the imagination are full.

One such story was reported by a man traveling alone to visit a friend. When he arrived by train at the station, there was no one to greet him, so rather than wait on the platform for someone to show up, he decided to set out on foot in the general direction of his friend's house. After walking through the countryside a while, he spied a well-lit house off in the distance and, thinking it the home of his friend, walked up the drive toward it. When he came close, he was greeted by a man who informed him that his friend's house was actually farther down the road, and proceeded to point the way. Thankful for the directions, the traveler left and eventually reached the home of his friend, where he recounted the day's events. His friend, however, became startled and responded that there were no houses between there and the station, only the ruins of a home that stood long ago. The next morning, to prove his point, the traveler led his host to the spot where he had seen the house the night before, only to find the ruined foundations of a house that no longer existed.

Phantom trains and disappearing farmhouses are not easily explained by the theories of telepathic impulses or residual hauntings, and finding a common theory that explains the various types of apparitions in this chapter seems almost impossible. How then are we to establish that they are even the same phenomenon if they differ so greatly? One theory that seems to come closest to providing an explanation for varying manifestations was developed by Dr. Robert Crookall, a British biologist, in the 1960s, and is known as the "vehicle of vitality." This theory states that there resides within us a "double" composed of a semi-physical, ectoplasmic material caught partially between this world and the next. When a person dies, especially by unnatural means, the shock can cause the ectoplasmic sheet to break away. Since it is ideoplastic—meaning it's formed by the dying person's thoughts or feelings—it may become whatever reflects the dying person's persona. Because it lies halfway between two worlds, it may even be capable of limited actions.

For some, apparitions are easy to dismiss and everything from insanity to outright fraud has been used as an excuse to discount their existence. Yet still they persist and the mountain of evidence grows even larger. I predict that it will become more difficult to continue to ignore the experiences of so many as researchers and compilers of apparition manifestations push forward with their studies. Much of the confusion over the years is due to the scientific community's labeling the phenomena as supernatural and paranormal. This effectively places the study of apparitions outside the field of reason and legitimacy, exiling it to the realm of children's tales not to be taken seriously by rational adults. What the evidence does show is that apparitions are not an accidental or random occurrence, but fall into a natural group or pattern. This is no more unnatural or "outside of normal" than gravity or the spherical nature of our planet. Yet often the discussion of apparitions brings snickers and amused looks from many—a reaction, I imagine, also experienced by visionaries such as Columbus, Newton, and Einstein.

In this chapter, we have examined the methodology of apparitions and a few of the mechanisms that may play a part in their manifestations. The process seems physiological in that it relies upon our senses—sight, hearing, touch, and even smell. The million-dollar question remains this, however: Are apparitions nothing more than the effects of a natural process, devoid of intelligence and purpose? Or are apparitions, at least in some forms, the spirits of human beings returned from the dead? At present, science offers us no clear answers.

Chapter 6

AMONG THE SPIRITS: GHOSTS

It would probably be more accurate to say that human beings are ghosts—ghosts with bodies.

— COLIN WILSON

*D*eath is just as difficult a concept for us today as it was for our ancestors centuries ago, and as time, culture, and technology have changed, so has our concept of death. For instance, not long ago, the moment an individual was declared dead depended on whether or not his or her body continued to breathe or the heart to beat. But with advances in medical technology, we now have machines that can keep a person's lungs and heart working long after all brain activity has ceased. So in 1968, a panel of distinguished doctors from Harvard Medical School met to redefine existing medical theories of death in light of changing technology and a better understanding of the human body. They decided that death as we know it today is a state in which a person's body suffers an irreversible cessation of all brain functions, including the brain stem. "Brain death" became the standard by which doctors and courts decided when an individual could be considered clinically dead. This definition can be somewhat misleading, however, because it portrays death as a single event rather than a process. But after the supply of oxygen-rich blood ceases to flow to the brain, its electrical impulses continue firing for an additional four minutes, the kidneys continue to function for another half hour, and the corneas of the eyes keep working for as long as six hours after the brain has died. Even after placing the body in the grave, fingernails and hair continue to grow until the body's molecules break down and eventually become dust.

For most of man's collective history, he has stood both captivated and terrified by the inevitability of this process. For some, death means the end of a brief existence, beyond which nothing remains but a dark, shapeless void. But for others death is seen as a new beginning as the person's life force or spirit survives to move on, in one form or another. Some believe that, once freed from the body, this spirit entity then inhabits whatever particular version of heaven or hell its culture believes in at the time. There are, however, some who believe that certain spirits find it difficult to move on to the next world and that, for one reason or another, they become confused or lost, or simply refuse to leave. These earthbound spirits are called ghosts and have come to be greatly feared for their ability to haunt the living.

Unlike the other forms of apparition manifestations discussed in the previous chapter, a belief in ghosts predates any of the theories concerning hallucinations, telepathic exchanges, or residual impressions that have become so popular today. In fact, not all that long ago, to suggest that what lurked about lonely crossroads or in dark attics was anything *other* than a ghost would have sounded ridiculous, and might have even gotten you stoned out of the village.

Contrary to this, Western science finds the belief in ghosts a hard pill to swallow. After all, science measures the world around it in observable, quantifiable facts and outcomes that can be consistently reproduced, while ghosts, on the other hand, have continually given a rather poor performance under such conditions. Ghosts don't seem willing to squeeze under a microscope or into a test tube for science to dissect and examine, but to say that a lack of willingness on the part of ghosts to be examined proves they do not exist would be erroneous, also.

One phenomenon being looked at more closely for answers to this dilemma is "deathbed visions." This occurs when a person suffering from a terminal illness or injury is visited by apparitions of deceased relatives or religious figures moments before his or her death. These apparitions are usually only visible to the dying person and are believed to come in order to comfort and guide them through their last moments. In most cases, the apparitions are well known to the person, but in other cases there may be no prior knowledge that the figures before them had already died—a fact that, when later revealed, provides strong veridical evidence of the experience. The impact of such visions is not generally known to frighten the person, but instead fills him or her with an overwhelming sense of peace and joy. So strong are the emotions experienced during the vision that the person typically loses all fear of dying and passes quite peacefully.

In 1926, one of the first serious studies of deathbed visions was published by Sir William Barrett, a prominent physicist and one of the founding fathers of the SPR. Barrett became interested in these visions after hearing an account from his wife, an obstetric surgeon at Mother's Hospital in Dublin, concerning a patient under her care who had recently died. According to Mrs. Barrett, the patient, referred to as Mrs. B, underwent a difficult pregnancy and, although the child was born safely, the mother barely clung to life. Surrounded by family and friends, Mrs. B lay in her hospital bed exhausted by her labor. Suddenly she began staring across the room as if transfixed and described a beautiful scene where beings of light slowly gathered around her bed. Then, as her face brightened, she exclaimed excitedly to those around her that her father and sister Vida had come to take her away. Although Mrs. B's father had died many years prior, she did not have any knowledge that her sister was also dead. The news of Vida's death three weeks prior had been kept from her, out of fear that the trauma would be too much in her fragile state. After conversing with the apparitions for a brief period, a look of happy resignation crossed Mrs. B's face. Turning to her husband and newborn child one last time, she said goodbye. Closing her eyes, she died smiling.

Impressed by eyewitness accounts of the incident and the veridical aspect of Mrs. B's dead sister's appearance, Barrett set out to collect accounts of similar visions, which he published in his famous work *Deathbed Visions: The Psychical Experiences of the Dying*. Many of the accounts he recorded showed striking parallels to one another, regardless of the dying person's social or economic status. Barrett found that some people in their last moments reported visions that he was convinced pointed to proof that life existed after death.

Unfortunately, Barrett died not long after the publication of his work, and so, too, did the interest in deathbed visions.

It wasn't until the 1960s that researchers began to take another look at this phenomenon when Dr. Karlis Osis of the American Society for Psychical Research (ASPR) suggested a study. An ambitious project to say the least, the study proposed to survey physicians and nurses in the United States and India to determine if deathbed visions were being reported among their patients. An undertaking of this nature, however, would require a great deal of funding—money the ASPR did not have at the time—and so the project was shelved until the 1970s, when the necessary funds suddenly appeared from a very unusual source.

To most of those who knew him, James Kidd appeared to be nothing more than an old scruffy prospector who spent his life staying in cheap hotels when he wasn't searching for gold in the mountains of Arizona. He was just another of the faceless men and women who ventured west to find their fortune with a pick and a miner's pan, but if James Kidd's life went unnoticed by most, then his death would certainly gain attention. In 1949, Kidd once again set off for the wilds of the mountains, but this time he never returned. Creditors convinced the courts to declare him legally dead in 1967 and open his safe-deposit box to pay his remaining debts. When the poor miner's box was finally opened, a surprise awaited the creditors. Sitting before them was a small fortune ($270,000 in cash and securities) and a will, scribbled in Kidd's own hand, leaving the entire sum to research that would prove the existence of life after death. Why a man like

Kidd chose a life of hardship when he possessed a comfortable fortune, or how he became interested in psychical research remain unanswered questions. But true to his wishes, after 130 contenders and years of litigation, Kidd's fortune finally found its way to the ASPR, and Osis was given the green light to launch his long-awaited study.

After interviewing thousands of physicians and nurses, Osis and his team found that not only were deathbed visions continuing to occur in the modern medical age, but also that their similarity to one another ruled out any possibility that they were isolated incidents. The study also explored whether the visions could be hallucinations brought on by fever, drugs, oxygen deprivation, or other physical trauma associated with dying. But after eliminating all the cases in which these elements may have been a factor, a sizeable number of cases remained where there was no biological explanation. In addition, unlike Sir William Barrett's earlier study that focused primarily on Anglo-European test subjects sharing the same cultural and religious expectations, Osis extended the range of his survey to include subjects from the country of India, whose primarily Hindu religious beliefs were very different from those of most Americans. Here too, he found evidence of deathbed visions among the population that could not be explained away as the product of a particular group's belief system. In the end, Osis felt the study's findings pointed in only one direction: that the phenomenon of deathbed visions was the result of contact with the spirit world.

Since that time, although interest in such visions has grown, researchers are finding it more and more difficult to collect accounts of them, due in part to the changing nature of health care. Under our modern system, when a person is about to die, he is usually confined to a hospital, hooked to various machines and tubes, and surrounded by medical staff he hardly knows. This is in direct contrast to earlier days, when people expected to die in the comfort of their own homes while being cared for by family members. Even worse, terminally ill patients today are often heavily sedated to help ease the painful physical symptoms of their passing, which makes communicating any last impressions extremely difficult. The sad truth of the matter is that with all our medical knowledge, we have not yet learned how to die.

Another phenomenon that lends weight to the belief in a spirit world is the occurrence of "out-of-body experiences" (OBE). This takes place when a person's spirit either leaves willingly or is forced out of the body through trauma or illness, and later returns fully conscious of the experience. One form of OBE is "astral projection," which occurs when a person either voluntarily, through proper breathing and relaxation, or spontaneously, without warning, projects his or her spirit outside of the body, remaining attached to the body by a long silver umbilical-like cord. This differs greatly from other accounts similar in nature to apparitions of the living, in that once freed from the body, the person is fully aware of his astral form and in complete control of its actions. During the experience, the person views his astral form as being roughly the same size, shape, and appearance as his material body. In this state, he is invisible to all others, and although he cannot manipulate objects, he can pass through solid matter, moving through walls and other structures with ease. After a period of time, the astral body is drawn back into the person's sleeping body by the silver cord connecting the two.

In the 1960s, Dr. Charles Tart, a psychologist at the University of California, began a series of experiments on subjects who claimed the ability to project their astral body voluntarily. Fitted with an electroencephalograph (EEG) to record the electrical activity of the brain, subjects were asked to lie down and bring themselves into a state of consciousness in which they could project their astral body. Once this was achieved, subjects were asked to perform a number of actions proving they had achieved an OBE. Tart's most productive subject was a woman he called Miss Z, who had since early childhood reported the ability to project her astral body voluntarily. During her experiments, a slip of paper with a random group of numbers and a digital clock showing the correct time were placed high on a shelf above her sleeping body. These could only be seen by Miss Z if she was successful in raising her astral body to a height close to the ceiling, above the shelf, where she could view the objects in question. By the fourth night of the experiments, Miss Z surprised her testers by repeating both the numbers on the paper and the correct time without physically stirring from her bed. In addition to these findings, Tart noted that during reported astral projection, test subjects demonstrated a loss of electrical brain activity that could not be accounted for in any sleeping or waking patterns known to science.

Decades before Tart's experiments in the United States, a discovery was made halfway around the world that may have given science an actual glimpse of this astral or spirit body. Behind the Soviet Iron Curtain, Russian electrical engineer Semyon Kirlian found in 1939 that if a living object was placed on a photographic plate and subjected to a high-frequency electric field, a radiating aura (normally invisible to the naked eye), could be seen surrounding it. When leaves from freshly cut plants were photographed in the same manner, they gave off brilliant auras that faded as the leaves died. This led Kirlian to conclude that the auras he captured on film were images of the life force or spirit that permeated all living things. Kirlian also found that each living thing had its own unique aura, which often changed color and composition to reflect its physical condition. For instance, there was a dramatic difference between the auras of healthy leaves and those infected with disease. Healthy leaves showed light-colored auras that pulsed and changed, while the sick leaves had darker colors, which radiated sluggishly. When humans were tested, not only did their auras change in relation to their physical state, but to their mental and emotional states as well. When an attractive member of the opposite sex entered the room, the aura of a test subject flared and changed rapidly, or if the subject was given a glass of alcohol to drink, the aura lit up like a fireworks display. For years the Soviet government dabbled with Kirlian photography as a means to maintain the health of their Olympic athletes, before eventually losing interest in its mixed results. The work of Semyon Kirlian might even have gone unnoticed altogether in the Western world, if not for the hard work of two American researchers, Sheila Ostrander and Lynn Schroeder, who introduced Kirlian's findings in the book *Psychic Discoveries Behind the Iron Curtain.*

Another form of OBE cited as proof of the spirit world is a phenomenon known as the near death experience (NDE). With advances in modern resuscitation techniques, physicians now have the ability, in some cases, to revive a person after he or she has been dead for a short period of time. Of those living through such an experience, some claim that at the moment of death, instead of slipping off into a dark oblivion of nothingness, they suddenly find themselves floating outside the body in the form of a spirit. Under these new conditions, they report that they can be neither seen nor heard by those around them, and actions as simple as grasping objects become impossible since their newly discovered spirit-body passes right through them. Despite their best efforts, they find that all they can do is to watch passively as doctors and paramedics fight to bring their body back to life—a scene which some are able to describe later in great detail, much to their physicians' astonishment. One such case comes from the testimony of a woman who died in her hospital bed and was later brought back to life through the efforts of the hospital staff:

> About a year ago, I was admitted to the hospital with heart trouble. The next morning, lying in the hospital bed, I began to have a very severe pain in my chest. I pushed the button beside the bed to call for the nurses, and they came in and started working on me. I was quite

uncomfortable lying on my back so I turned over, and as I did I quit breathing and my heart stopped beating. Just then, I heard the nurses shout, "Code pink! Code pink!" As they were saying this, I could feel myself moving out of my body and sliding down between the mattresses and the rail on the side of the bed—actually it seemed as if I went through the rail—and on down to the floor. Then I started rising upward, slowly. On my way up, I saw more nurses come running into the room—there must have been a dozen of them. My doctor happened to be making his rounds in the hospital, so they called him and I saw him come in, too. I thought, "I wonder what he's doing here." I drifted on up past the light fixture—saw it from the side and very distinctly—and then I stopped, floating right below the ceiling, looking down. I felt almost as though I were a piece of paper that someone had blown to the ceiling. I watched them reviving me from up there! My body was lying down there, stretched out on the bed in plain view, and they were all standing around it. I heard one nurse say, "Oh, my God! She's gone!" while another one leaned down to give me mouth-to-mouth resuscitation. I was looking down at the back of her head while she did this. I'll never forget the way her hair looked; it was cut kind of short. Just then, I saw them roll this machine in there, and they put the shocks on my chest. When they did, I saw my whole body just jump right off the bed, and I heard every bone in my body crack and pop. It was the most awful thing! As I saw them below, beating on my chest and rubbing my arms and legs, I thought, "Why are they going to so much trouble? I'm just fine now" (Moody 1976, 34–35).

After a brief period in this disconnected state, others report that they become aware of an uncomfortable buzzing, which grows louder and louder until they find themselves drawn away from their body at great speed through a dark tunnel toward a bright light. While journeying through the darkness, they are approached by the spirits of family and friends who have already died. Much like the apparitions reported in deathbed visions, these spirits play a comforting and guiding role as the person moves closer to his destination in the light. Some of these figures the person may have known during his lifetime, while others are only recognized after the experience from family histories or old photos. Nevertheless, once the person reaches the light, he somehow knows that within it lies a barrier between the world of the living and the dead, and to cross it means never to return. At this point, a being of light, very different from the other spirits encountered so far, approaches; it is often associated with an important religious figure such as Jesus Christ or a particular saint. The being then prompts the person to examine his life by flashing before him a panoramic view of mental pictures, replaying his entire living experience. After the review, most people feel a strong desire to pass through the barrier and discover what awaits them on the other side. Before this can happen, however, something stops them and they are either commanded to return by the being of light or suddenly feel a pulling sensation, which drags them back into their body. Usually, the return is against their will, but no matter how hard they resist, they find themselves back in the heavy and painful world of their material body.

Although NDEs have become increasingly widespread in recent years with more people coming forward to share their experiences, there is evidence to be found within various cultures' myths and legends throughout history to suggest that NDEs are not merely a modern occurrence. The famous Sioux medicine man, Black Elk, once told the story of a powerful vision he received as a young child. One day when Black Elk was still a small boy of only nine winters, he grew sick and was confined to a pony drag as the tribe moved from one hunting ground to another. His face and limbs swelled horribly and he wavered in and out of consciousness as his small body lay racked with fever. During one of these spells, he lay in his father's teepee looking up through the smoke hole at the sky above, when suddenly he found himself outside of his body, being led into the clouds by spirit guides who showed him many powerful visions. At times, looking down on his own body, he watched the tribe's medicine man chant and pray over him while his family mourned. After twelve days among the spirits, his guides came to him and told him that it was time for him to return to his people, and before he knew it he was again in his body. In a few days his illness disappeared as quickly as it came and Black Elk grew to be a leader among his tribe, never forgetting the visions he witnessed in the clouds.

In Black Elk's story we find a series of elements common to other tales from various cultures throughout history. Although his visions were overlaid with the Native American belief system that he was accustomed to, it would take no great stretch of imagination to redefine the experience in a context more familiar to our modern way of thinking. Spirit guides could easily become apparitions of loved ones, the prayers of the medicine man could be seen as similar to a doctor's attempts at resuscitation, and the powerful visions described by Black Elk sound much like the "life review" many survivors describe. The parallels between today's NDEs and similar tales from the past are striking, to say the least, and the comparisons could go on and on.

After interviewing hundreds of patients who have experienced an NDE, Dr. Raymond Moody—the man who coined the term "near death experience" and a pioneer in the field—identified a series of steps associated with this phenomenon:

1) The person suddenly finds him- or herself outside of the body, watching attempts to resuscitate it.

2) After a period of time, an uncomfortable sound begins, described by some as a sort of buzzing noise, by others as strange but beautiful music.

3) Concurrent with this noise, the person feels as though he is moving away from the scene of his death through a dark place toward a light.

4) Along the dark journey, beings appear in the form of deceased friends and relatives to guide and comfort the person.

5) Drawn to the light, the person comes to understand that what lies beyond him is a barrier that separates the world of the living from that of the dead.

6) While in the light, the person is approached by a being unlike any he has encountered so far. This figure prompts him to examine his life through a series of mental pictures.

7) At this point, or sometimes at an earlier stage, the person is told that he must return to the world of the living, and feels pulled back into his body.

Moody was careful to point out that, although these stages were a rough outline of events, they in no way reflected the experience in its entirety. Some NDEs involved only a few of the stages and not always in the same order. The number of the stages encountered or the depth of the NDE often depended on the length of time the person was reported to have remained dead. The longer the person remained dead, the deeper and more detailed the NDE seemed to be. In addition, the experience proved to be difficult for many people to place into words properly, as if the images and emotions associated with the afterlife encounter were beyond the reach of human vocabulary. Many struggled to make sense of the event and, like Black Elk, placed it in terms and imagery that they could understand. Dr. Moody also noticed that none of the experiences involved the classical images of hell and punishment that some believe await them for their misdeeds. On the contrary, those who have returned recount feelings of love and acceptance far beyond anything they had experienced before. Many even claim a reluctance to return to their bodies and resent the efforts of those who resuscitated them.

For most NDE survivors, however, the proof of their experience lies not in physical evidence or statistical data, but in the effect that it has on their lives. Many come to believe that their encounter with death has given them a greater sense of purpose and a deeper form of spirituality. This transformation often allows survivors to overcome the fear of death that they once clung to and replace it with the assurance that what lies beyond the realm of life is not the end of existence, but the beginning of something new. After Black Elk's visions, he went on to become a powerful leader among his people, inspired by the lessons he was taught when he walked among the spirits.

If the evidence supplied by phenomena such as deathbed visions and NDEs is to be taken at face value, then what lies beyond death is not a dark void of nonexistence, but rather a world of beauty and light filled with the familiar faces of those who have gone before us. Yet, if our spirits can look forward to such an appealing place after death, then why do some return to haunt the living in the form of ghosts? This is an important question, because understanding what motivates them to remain in an earthbound state will show just how they differ from other forms of apparitions.

In many hauntings, apparitions seem content to wander the centuries through scenery that no longer exists, passing through walls that once held doors or floating up staircases long since fallen. In hauntings involving ghosts, however, there is a much stronger degree of awareness and motivation in the manifestations. Ghosts have been recorded playing tricks, manipulating objects, answering questions posed to them (although not always telling the truth), and even cracking a joke or two. At times, the distinctions between a ghost and an apparition can become blurry and overlap, but for the most part apparitions have the mechanical personality of a cardboard character from a bad novel rather than the well-rounded intelligence displayed by ghosts. In short, ghosts exhibit a degree of depth and complexity and a capacity for interaction not found in their apparitional counterparts. This has led many to conclude that the nature of a person changes very little after death. Once freed from the body, ghosts consist of everything that once made them individuals when still alive. All the thoughts, feelings, memories, and desires that make us unique in this world carry over to the next. Therefore, if a person lived a violent life filled with turmoil and anger, he may find himself plagued by the same negative emotions after death. Only this time, things are a little trickier as he struggles in a world where he no longer has a material body in which to interact with those around him. If his emotional baggage is heavy enough, it can bind the ghost, cursing it to haunt the land of the living.

In order to understand the process better, it's important to examine a few of the more famous cases throughout history that demonstrate the motivation and intelligence that points to ghosts as the source of the hauntings. One such example comes not from the archives of some famed ghost hunter, but first appeared in the most unlikely of places—a 1974 newsletter of the U.S. Flight Safety Foundation.

On the night of December 29, 1972, Eastern Airlines Flight 401 crashed into the Florida Everglades outside of

Miami International Airport. The Lockheed L-1011 TriStar was part of a then-new line of jumbo jets termed "whisper-liners" and was considered a masterpiece of modern engineering. Shortly before the crash and on final approach to the airport, the flight crew radioed the Miami control tower to report difficulty with the jet's forward landing gear. The tower instructed them to abort the approach and go around in order to troubleshoot the problem. While circling over the dark waters of the Everglades, Flight 401 slowly descended until it plowed into the swamps, ripping itself apart. More than one hundred passengers and crew members died that fateful night, some of whom survived the impact only to drown in the swamp's black waters, still buckled to their seats. The horror of the crash shocked the nation and for weeks grisly photos made front-page news. An investigation by the Federal Aviation Administration and Eastern Airlines eventually determined the crash to be a result of pilot error related to unintentional disengagement of the autopilot system, and laid the matter to rest.

But if airline officials thought they had closed the book on Flight 401, they were mistaken. Not long after the crash, rumors began to circulate among airline crews that the ghosts of two dead crewmembers from Flight 401, Captain Robert Loft and Flight Engineer Don Repo, were haunting Eastern flights. Most reported seeing the ghosts as full-bodied figures in flight uniforms; at times they were even mistaken for living crew members—that is, until the moment they disappeared right in front of a startled witness's eyes. During each appearance, both ghosts seemed in some way concerned with the operation or safety of the plane they were haunting. For instance, on one occasion a flight captain reported that while performing a preflight check before take-off, he entered the plane's flight deck and found another pilot in his seat who turned and said, "You don't have to worry about the preflight. I've already done it." The figure then vanished before the startled captain, who later recognized the man from a photograph: it was Don Repo. During another sighting of Repo, his ghost warned a flight crew that the plane would experience electrical failure while in flight. When the captain called for a second check of the plane's flight systems, it was discovered that there was a faulty electrical circuit in the instrument panel.

These appearances weren't limited to Eastern Airline crews, and it wasn't long before passengers also began to report encountering the ghostly duo. Right before the start of one flight, a voice came over the plane's intercom announcing the customary seat belt instructions and other preflight precautions. As the passengers began to comply with the request, the crew stood stunned. The intercom system wasn't on and several crewmembers recognized the voice as belonging to the deceased Captain Robert Loft. Other manifestations, however, didn't go over so well and one passenger became so upset when the ghost of Don Repo appeared next to her out of thin air that she became hysterical and had to be removed by police when the plane landed.

As news of the sightings leaked to the general public, Eastern Airlines attempted to stifle the rumors out of concern that being labeled a "haunted airline" would hurt profits. Flight logs recounting the appearances disappeared and crewmembers that came forward with such tales were threatened, first with a visit to the company shrink, and then with unemployment. Further, officials noted that the ghosts were only sighted on those planes that had been fitted with parts salvaged from the doomed aircraft. So in what must have been a rather costly overhaul, Eastern took steps to remove all the salvaged parts from its planes. After this, the ghosts of Captain Robert Loft and Flight Engineer Don Repo were never reported seen again.

Exactly why the ghosts of Flight 401 stopped manifesting is difficult to say. Were they in some way linked to the salvaged parts from their doomed flight, or did they return to complete a job they never finished while alive? In all the manifestations, both ghosts seemed concerned with the safety of the plane on which they appeared, as if to make sure that the tragedy that befell them that dark night over the Everglades was never repeated. Guilt can be a very strong emotion, and perhaps as their spirits passed from their dying bodies that chaotic night, their last thoughts turned to the lives lost under their care. Powerful feelings such as these could trap the pair of ghosts on the physical plane until they felt they had in some way made amends by watching over the passengers and crews on other aircraft. But whatever the reason for their return, many Eastern pilots and crew thought of their presence as a good luck charm. After all, it's good to have a wingman watching your tail, even if it is a ghost.

One story often cited as proof of the existence of ghosts comes from the files of the SPR when, in 1921, they investigated the case of James Chaffin, a simple farmer from North Carolina. When Chaffin died, his will left all of his earthly possessions to his eldest son Marshall, which of course didn't sit very well with his surviving wife and three additional sons, who stood to receive nothing. Then one night, four years after his father's death, James Jr. awoke from a disturbing dream that changed everything. In the dream, his father stood by James's bed, dressed in his usual old black coat and looking remorseful. Leaning close to his son, the ghost said that the will James's older brother Marshall possessed was not the last true copy. The last will and testament outlining his true intentions, he explained, could be found in the pocket of the old coat like the one he wore in the dream. The next day James Jr. quickly tracked the coat to his brother John's house. In its pocket the two found a note written by their father before his death, which read, "Read the 27th chapter of Genesis in my daddy's old Bible." After racing to find the family Bible, the two brothers opened the large book as directed to find folded within its pages a will hand-written by their father, which postdated the one their brother Marshall possessed. Initially Marshall contested the new will, which divided the estate evenly among all the family members, but in the end he admitted the will appeared genuine and the estate was redistributed accordingly. There were many twists and turns to this rather extraordinary case and investigators with the SPR found it hard to dispute the veridical nature of James Jr.'s dream. After the redistribution of the estate, James Chaffin Sr. was never seen again by his son James Jr., or anyone else. Perhaps once his earthly business was finished and his family was provided for, he could rest in peace.

Another ghost unable to rest quietly until it had resolved unfinished business seemed determined to clear its name. The official report from the United States Naval Academy at Annapolis, Maryland, read that on the night of October 13, 1907, Lieutenant James Sutton committed suicide with his own pistol. Witnesses testified that earlier that night, Lt. Sutton attended a dance where he was seen drinking heavily. Afterward, he returned to base with friends, where a fight erupted and he was thrown to the ground. Enraged by the offense, Sutton threatened to kill everyone present and stumbled off to his tent to retrieve his pistol. By then the authorities had been notified and, spotting Sutton leaving his tent with a firearm, they moved to arrest him. Another fight broke out when they tried to disarm him and it was reported that, before he could be stopped, Sutton deliberately placed the gun to his head and ended his own life. That, of course, was the official version of events as released by the military; however, there remains another side to the story, told by someone no one expected to hear from again.

On the other side of the country, in Portland, Oregon, Sutton's mother was receiving the terrible news of her son's death when his ghostly figure suddenly appeared before her. It said, "Momma, I never killed myself. . . . My hands are as free from blood as when I was five years old." The ghost went on to claim that others had killed him and that his death was being made to look like a suicide. For the next few months, James's ghost continued to visit Mrs. Sutton both in her dreams and while awake, each time pleading for her to believe that he was murdered. During each brief visit, lasting no more than a minute or two, he provided important details about the fight and the wounds he received at the hands of his murderers. This was information that, at the time, Mrs. Sutton had no access to, which was only later verified during an investigation.

With nowhere else to turn for help, Mrs. Sutton was eventually able to convince the ASPR to investigate her son's ghostly appearances. Given that the only remaining evidence lay buried in a grave in Arlington National Cemetery, investigators had Sutton's body exhumed. Upon examining his battered, decomposing corpse, wounds were discovered that did not appear in the original Navy doctor's autopsy, evidence of great physical trauma consistent with the information provided by Sutton's ghost. Investigators were stunned by the accuracy of the information and began to seriously doubt claims by the Navy that Sutton had committed suicide. There were other problems with the Navy's version of events as well. Glaring discrepancies in the testimonies of the witnesses began to surface and it seemed as if many crucial facts were being either overlooked or simply ignored by the Navy.

Over time, Sutton's ghost returned less frequently until the manifestations stopped altogether. Perhaps it was the reopening of the case by the military that allowed him to move on, or maybe he just had something to say and refused to leave until those close to him were convinced of his innocence. Although the ASPR found that the veridical information provided by Sutton's ghost gave weight and credibility to claims that he had returned from the dead to clear his name, the Navy was not convinced. To this day, the death of Lt. James Sutton remains "officially" unresolved.

As we learned in earlier chapters, many cultures went to great lengths to ensure that the bodies of the dead were disposed of properly and with respect. The Greeks were no exception to the belief that ghosts of the dead took an active interest in the way their bodies were cared for. If done improperly, a ghost could return and haunt the spot until the offense was righted. One such story handed down through the ages has become something of a classic in the literature of ghost lore, and although it may sound anecdotal and somewhat clichéd, it serves to demonstrate the lengths to which ghosts are thought to go in order to communicate their plight to the living.

In the first century CE, the famous historian Pliny the Younger wrote to his patron Lucias Sura about a haunting he believed to be true beyond all doubt. His tale began in the city of Athens where a certain old house, long abandoned, had gained a sinister reputation. There were rumors among the citizens that on some nights the sounds of heavy chains could be heard rattling from inside. Those souls brave enough to venture into the house on such nights quickly returned with tales of a ghost described by Pliny as "the very picture of abject filth and misery. His beard was long and matted, his white hair disheveled and unkempt.

His thin legs were loaded with a weight of galling fetters that he dragged wearily along with a painful moaning; his wrists were shackled by long cruel links, while ever and anon he raised his arms and shook his shackles in a kind of impotent fury" (Cohen 1984, 39). Of course, with this sort of reputation, the house remained unoccupied and in time fell into disrepair.

The house would have fallen into complete ruin if it wasn't for a philosopher named Athenodorus, who wandered into the city looking for a place to live. At the time, Athenodorus was very poor and, not having heard the rumors of the horrible chain-rattling ghost, rented the place very cheaply. On his very first night in his new place, the philosopher sat deeply absorbed in his studies when he heard the faint rattling of chains. Initially, Athenodorus refused to be bothered by the noise, but as time wore on, the rattling grew louder until it could be ignored no longer. Looking up, Athenodorus found himself staring into the face of a ghastly figure draped in chains, beckoning to him. So with what must have been a great deal of courage, he picked up his small oil lamp and followed the ghost as it led him through the house and into the adjoining garden. There, among the overgrown tangle of bushes and vines, the ghost stopped, looked sadly at the ground, and gestured to the spot before vanishing.

The next day, Athenodorus led authorities to the place in the garden the ghost had indicated and, after digging only a few feet into the soft earth, they uncovered the remains of a human skeleton wrapped in chains—the source of the haunting. The remains were given a proper burial according to Athenian custom and the house was cleansed of any lingering influences with magical rituals. After these measures, Pliny writes that the ghost of the unknown man was never seen again and that Athenodorus could finally study undisturbed.

Some ghosts, like the one described by Pliny, can haunt an area for many years trapped within their own tragedy, while others have been known to return briefly, unable to move on until they've said goodbye. These may be the most frequently encountered ghosts and appear much like the crisis apparitions discussed in chapter five. Probably one of the best illustrations of this from our own time involves the tale of a lovable little ghost named Bounce.

While Miss Grazebrook was staying with her sister in Norfolk one summer, she took notice of a stray dog the family had adopted and named Bounce. It was an ugly mongrel and so got little attention or petting compared to the other, better-looking dogs around the house. Despite these shortcomings, Miss Grazebrook took pity on the poor animal and showered him with affection and even a few table scraps. In return, Bounce became devoted to her and spent as much time at her heels as possible. As her summer with the family drew to a close, Miss Grazebrook returned home, in time forgetting all about little Bounce—that is, until he came to visit one last time. One night, as she lay sleeping, she was awakened by the sound of a dog barking in her room. Sitting up, she was bewildered to find Bounce sitting next to her bed. Reaching over to pet him, she asked sleepily, "Bounce, how did you get here?" Then in what she could only describe as the sound of a human voice inside her head, Bounce responded, "I was shot yesterday. I have come to say goodbye," and vanished (Stirling 1958, 131–32). The next morning, when she told the rest of her family about what she had seen, they laughed and told her that she must have been dreaming. Six weeks later, however, she learned just how wrong they were when a letter arrived from her sister's governess, in which she mentioned that the family had moved and, since they could find no home for poor Bounce, they felt it better to shoot him. This had occurred only a few days before Miss Grazebrook had encountered Bounce in her bedroom. Bounce, it seemed, had come to thank a friend for her kindness and to say goodbye.

The reasons why ghosts return are as complex and as varied as the human story itself. Some return out of love, others out of hate; some come back to right a wrong or to seek revenge, and some just want to say goodbye before they go. Some of their tales can be found in the countless books on the subject that fill library shelves, others we tell to frighten each other as we huddle around the fireplace on cold dark nights, and finally, some still wait to be discovered, as silent and as unseen as ghosts themselves.

Whatever ghosts' reasons for returning, those who find themselves in the unique position of experiencing a haunting firsthand generally react in one of two ways. First, some people respond with a degree of curiosity and even compassion. These people are usually open-minded enough to accept the manifestations going on around them and readily come to terms with the experience. Some people may even welcome an otherworldly encounter. In some cultures, ghosts are jealously guarded by a family as an important part of its history. The owners of many an English manor or Southern plantation house prided themselves as much on the ghosts who haunted the grounds as on its architecture or history. Today, interest in visiting haunted places is growing, and the waiting list at some well-publicized haunted bed and breakfasts can be a year long.

At the other end of the spectrum are those who find their ghostly encounter a truly terrifying experience. Many of these people develop the attitude that "this house isn't big enough for the both of us" and turn to such drastic measures as religious exorcisms to clean their house of what they consider "evil spirits." These ancient rituals vary from culture to culture, but are primarily designed to violently expel a trapped spirit. In many cases, however, this approach can backfire because ghosts are not demons and cannot be intimidated by spiritual bullying. Instead, they can become very upset at being threatened and strike back by increasing the intensity of the haunting. In the long run, families that refuse to accept the fact that they share their home with an invisible guest (or guests!) usually end up looking for another place to live. After all, in most cases, the ghost was there first anyway.

Given these various reactions, a debate has been growing among scientists and amateur ghost enthusiasts alike. Once you have a ghost, so to speak, what do you do with it? Many researchers believe that ghosts should be observed and tested, as if they were some form of spiritual lab rat. Others believe that ghosts are not a phenomenon to be studied, like gravity or cold fusion; rather, they should be treated as sentient beings that need our help. This has led to the development of an approach known as spirit releasement.

The technique originated during the Spiritualist movement of the early twentieth century, although similar practices are known to have existed among primitive peoples. A Spiritualist church known as The Temple of Light in Kansas City, Missouri, began developing ways to use mediums to communicate with ghosts, to convince them that they needed to end their haunting and move on to a higher plain of existence where they could find happiness. The organization also believed that many mental illnesses were the result of a ghost's attempts to influence a person, and prescribed spirit releasement for disorders ranging from schizophrenia to depression. The key to mental illness, they believed, was not to be found on a psychiatrist's couch, but in the séance room, where the ghost, not the living person, was the true patient.

Since that time, the process has been refined and has shed many of its Spiritualist trappings. Those who practice spirit releasement claim that it is simply a matter of opening the lines of communication between themselves and the ghost. This usually occurs at the site of the haunting, although some mediums claim to be able to release a ghost from a distance through a form of mental telepathy. In either case, the first step is to successfully establish contact with the ghost, which can be difficult if the ghost is reluctant to talk or afraid of being discovered. Once a dialogue has been established, the medium attempts to understand who the ghost is and why it feels bound to the location of the haunting. Knowing what is keeping the ghost trapped in its earthbound state can help the medium coax it into facing the issues that are keeping it there. In some cases, ghosts may first have to be convinced that they are truly dead. If this doesn't work, the medium may ask other spirits familiar to the ghost, such as deceased friends and relatives it might have known while alive, to step in and lead the ghost into the spirit world. There are those who claim that spirit releasement can be accomplished by anyone through prayers or by simply asking the ghost to leave in a polite but firm voice. Others feel that the task can only be handled by a sensitive medium trained in the procedure. Either way, ghosts cannot be forced to go and must leave willingly. In the end, if the ties that bind them to the location are too strong, there is little that actually can be done.

———◦———

In the vast collection of stories and case studies dealing with apparition manifestations, we find that some can only be explained in light of the theory that ghosts are real. If such is the case, then there exists a group of spirits trapped in a sort of limbo between the worlds of the living and the dead, and it is our duty to treat them with respect and compassion. After all, one day it could be you.

So far we have explored the realms of apparitions and ghosts, examining both their likenesses and differences.

Next we will move on to an associated phenomenon—the poltergeist. As you will learn, poltergeists are an entirely different matter.

Chapter 7

"They're Here": Poltergeists

A ghost haunts; a poltergeist infests.
— Harry Price

At first glance, the phenomenon of the poltergeist appears so similar to what occurs during manifestations of apparitions and ghosts that it can be difficult to tell one from the other. On the surface, we find that all three involve strange noises, moving objects, and ghostly figures, but if we dig deeper we begin to unearth facts that show the differences becoming more and more pronounced. Unlike its close cousins the ghost and the apparition, the poltergeist is a noisy, mischievous, destructive entity prone to acts of mindless violence. Typically these juvenile antics encompass phenomena such as showers of stones, unexplained fires, and loud frightening noises that mimic the sounds of explosions or rumbling thunder. Although its pranks may seem real, they rarely damage the objects or injure those they are directed at. For instance, from a room may come the sounds of furniture being horribly smashed about, but upon investigation the room is found intact with no signs of anything being out of place.

The term "poltergeist" is a combination of two German words: the verb *polter* means to make loud noises by knocking or throwing things about, while the noun *geist* translates into the word for ghost. The Germans' concept of the poltergeist was similar to that of a ghost, but unlike the average run-of-the-mill *geist* known to haunt dark forests and old castles, the poltergeist delights in rampant noise-making and destruction. The *polterabend*, as it's known, occurs on the night of a wedding when friends of the bride and the groom gather at the couple's home to celebrate. As the newlyweds retire for the evening, their drunken guests smash bottles, break china, and destroy as much cookery as possible. The racket made by the guests symbolizes the breaking of the couple's bonds to friends and family—rambunctious behavior not unlike that of the poltergeist.

One of the first written accounts of a poltergeist showed up in an eighth-century manuscript that recounted the tale of a farmhouse in Bingen, Germany, on the Rhine River, that was plagued by an "evil spirit" that threw rocks, shook walls, and burned crops. As if this weren't enough, the invisible entity followed the farmer wherever he went, accusing him of some rather embarrassing activities, including sleeping with his overseer's daughter—a claim, I'm sure, the overseer did not find very amusing. Under constant bombardment from the evil spirit, the farmer soon found that his friends and neighbors were shunning him, fearing that they too might suffer the wrath of the spirit. Finally, the Bishop of Mainz was called in to perform the necessary rites to banish the spirit. A long session of hymn singing and holy-water sprinkling followed, but the tale ends without mentioning whether the exorcism worked.

Evil spirits such as the one at Bingen were well known throughout Europe and other parts of the world, with similar tales found from as far away as China. Generally the mischief was looked at as no more than an unsettling experience, easily handled by the proper amulet or priestly exorcism. But by the dawn of the sixteenth century, such experiences began to be taken more seriously, eventually considered to be the work of the devil and his covens of witches. By this time, the Protestant Reformation was in full swing as the church strove to purge its flock of pagan superstitions and to assert itself as a centralized authority in a time of warfare, famine, and plague. The backlash created a wave of mass hysteria that spread across Europe and the American Colonies, culminating in the deaths of thousands of innocent men and women. It's impossible to determine how many of those thought to be possessed by demons or burned at the stake for witchcraft were merely the victims of poltergeist activity. However, an examination of some trial records from this period shows phenomena identical to what occurs in poltergeist cases.

In 1661, two particular cases drew the attention of Joseph Glanvill, chaplain to King Charles II, who published their accounts in 1682 in his book *Sadducismus Triumphatus*. The first involved Florence Newton, who was brought before the court for bewitching a maidservant, Mary Longdon, on March 24 in Cork, England. Mary claimed that when she refused to give Florence some meat from her master's pantry, Florence flew into a rage and placed a curse on her. Mary said that, not long after the confrontation, she was tormented by grotesque apparitions and showers of stones that fell upon her even while indoors. Many others, including her master, testified to these events, adding that Mary would sometimes vomit pins and needles. One night a spirit even transported her from her bed to the roof of her master's house. Apparently the court was impressed with the testimony against Florence and sentenced her to prison—a slap on the hand when compared to the usual sentence of torture and burning.

Glanvill also relates what is considered to be one of the best-documented studies available of early poltergeist activity. At the same time that Florence Newton was being tried for witchcraft, William Drury marched into the town of Ludgarshall, near Tedworth, England, with only an old drum, begging for alms. Drury was a rather colorful character and, after failing to con the town's bailiff out of money with phony documents, he stomped about, beating his drum in protest. He made so much noise that the magistrate, John Mompesson, had him jailed for disturbing the peace. Drury pleaded his case, but the magistrate was in no mood for nonsense. Although he released Drury, he confiscated the drum, which remained at Mompesson's house for safekeeping.

Yet if the magistrate thought that with the vagrant drummer gone things would return to normal, he was sadly mistaken. One month later, while Mompesson was away on business, his family was awakened one night by loud banging noises from within the house that sounded much like the beating of a drum. A search of the house offered no clue to its source, but night after night it continued, growing so loud that soon the neighbors were complaining of the noise. By the time Mompesson returned home to his terrified family, the activity had grown beyond just nocturnal drumming. The sounds increased to include grunting and scratching from within the walls and ceiling, chamber pots were emptied onto the beds, and the servants began reporting seeing a black figure with glowing red eyes. People within the household also became targets of the entity, as servants were chased around with sticks and children torn from their beds at night by an invisible force. Mompesson destroyed the drum, hoping to end the terror, but the activity only increased, becoming more and more violent. The household began to fall apart under the constant pressure and servants quit in fear.

While these bizarre events were occurring at the magistrate's home, Drury found himself in trouble again in a town not too far from Tedworth. This time the charge was pig stealing, which carried with it a sentence of deportation to the American Colonies. However, while in jail waiting for the prison ship, he managed to escape and made his way back to Tedworth, where he bought another drum and promptly began beating it in the town square. Again he was arrested, but this time instead of being charged with disturbing the peace, he was charged with the much more serious offense of bewitching the magistrate's home. Undaunted by the events, Drury not only confessed to the charge, but also boasted of his mystical powers to the other prisoners. Despite this confession, Drury was acquitted of witchcraft and charged again with pig stealing. Sentenced once again to deportation, he was shipped out on the next available prison ship. This time, William Drury, the Drummer of Tedworth, was never heard from again. Interestingly enough, as soon as Drury disappeared, the spirit rampaging about John Mompesson's home did so as well.

During these strange events, Reverend Glanvill did his best to investigate the matter as thoroughly as possible, going to great lengths to interview witnesses and observe phenomena himself. At one point, he even considered the possibility that trickery and fraud might be involved and recounted a particularly telling incident reported to him by John Mompesson. It appears that one evening Mompesson observed pieces of wood moving by themselves in the chimney room. Grabbing his pistol, Mompesson fired at the wood, halting its movement. When the house was searched, blood was found in the chimney room, on the stairs, and in several other locations around the house. No one admitted faking the activity, nor was the wounded person ever found. Yet, regardless of how carefully Glanvill investigated the matter, he was still a man of his time and a man of the clergy. The final report read that the occurrences in the home of John Mompesson were the work of bewitchment: a verdict that was all too often stamped on poltergeist activity for centuries thereafter.

This sinister image of poltergeists lasted until the late nineteenth century, when members of the Spiritualist movement claimed that phenomena linked to this activity were the work of returning spirits and not the devil or his minions. To support this belief, Spiritualists proclaimed that the phenomena found in poltergeist cases were identical to what transpired in the darkness of the séance room. In both instances, objects appeared, disappeared, or moved unassisted, disembodied voices called out, and explosive raps or noises sounded. In addition, many of the poltergeists that communicated to witnesses claimed actually to be spirits of the dead. Therefore, since they looked, sounded, and acted alike, Spiritualists reasoned that they must be one and the same.

One example of this new assertion occurred in 1926, when famed English ghost hunter Harry Price traveled to Vienna to observe the mediumistic powers of a thirteen-year-old girl named Eleonore Zugun. Born in the small rural village of Talpa, Romania, she started exhibiting otherworldly powers around the age of twelve, when a shower of stones fell upon her inside her family's cottage. The highly superstitious residents of the hamlet claimed that she was bewitched and, when phenomena such as moving objects and raps followed, they promptly shipped her off to the nearby Convent of Gorovei. Exorcisms followed, as well as visits to hospitals and psychiatrists, until a Romanian woman interested in Spiritualism, Countess Wassilko-Serecki, rescued Zugun from an insane asylum. Labeled "the poltergeist girl" by the popular press, Zugun conducted sittings for the wealthy, demonstrating powers that her new guardians touted as being from beyond the grave. Contrary to this, however, Harry Price's investigation revealed a child suffering from a poltergeist attack rather than exhibiting mediumistic powers. Zugun could not control the phenomena occurring around her and was at times the target of it. Throughout her time as a medium, she suffered from a particular stigmata that caused painful-looking teeth marks to appear on her body, which she blamed on *Dracu*, the devil.

It appears that Spiritualists of the time were rather talented at selective reasoning and generally ignored the fact that although phenomena in the séance room were easily controlled by the mediums, poltergeists were an entirely different matter. Like an ill-mannered child, the poltergeist appeared when it wanted, did what it wanted and, unlike the cooperative spirit guides of the mediums, could be very cruel. Although many poltergeists claimed to have once been alive, they have also claimed to be angels, demons, persons who are actually still living, and even aliens from outer space. These identities rarely held up under close scrutiny and, once caught in the lie, the poltergeist often simply switched to a new one with almost childish glee.

As scientists and researchers began investigating the claims made by mediums, they also turned their attention to poltergeist phenomena. But proving whether a medium was genuine was nothing like trying to wrangle a poltergeist into a laboratory. Time and again investigators would encounter an entity that had the tricky habit of manifesting just outside the range of their cameras and other instruments. In other cases, poltergeist manifestations ceased as soon as investigators arrived, only to begin again with renewed energy after they left. Because of this elusiveness, many investigators shied away from poltergeists, thinking that those reporting them were merely faking the manifestations as a form of attention-seeking. The game of cat and mouse made studying the poltergeist a frustrating task—a game the poltergeist seemed to enjoy a great deal.

In the 1970s, parapsychologist William G. Roll created a profile of the poltergeist experience taken from cases ranging from 1612 to 1974. In most cases, he discovered that there existed a strong relationship between the entity and its victim. Unlike a traditional haunting, poltergeists appeared not to be bound by a particular location or event. Instead, people seemed to attract them most. Usually these were adolescents who suddenly found themselves the center of the manifestation, termed the "agent" or "focus" of the activity. Roll also noticed that, because of this relationship, the strength and nature of the poltergeist manifestation was in many ways determined by the focus. For instance, the farther away from the activity the focus was, the less likely a manifestation was to occur. If the focus were to travel, say to a relative's home some distance away, then the poltergeist activity would suddenly stop at the previous location and, in many cases, would follow the focus to the relative's home where it would begin anew (Guiley 1992, 324).

One case examined by Roll, which helped him to understand the nature of this strange relationship, began in 1878, in the small town of Amherst, Nova Scotia. Esther and Jennie Cox lived with their older sister and her husband, Olive and Daniel Teed. When the two girls were startled awake one night, they swore there was a mouse moving around in their mattress or under the bed. When they pulled a box from underneath the bed, they found no mice, but the box seemed to have a mind of its own and flew into the air. Several nights later Jennie was awakened again, but this time by the sounds of nineteen-year-old Esther moaning as if she were dying. Reaching over to examine her with a lamp, Jennie screamed in horror. Esther lay in the bed, her body swelling to nearly twice its normal size, eyes bulging from their sockets, hair standing on end as if electricity were passing through it. At the sound of Jennie's screams, the rest of the family flooded into the room and were rocked by three loud booms that shook the house like thunderbolts. Bewildered by what was happening, the family watched as Esther's body returned to its normal state. The next night the house again rumbled with the deep sounds of thunder as Esther's horrible swelling returned and pillows and covers from her bed flew around the room as if hurled by an invisible entity.

Having nowhere else to turn, the family physician, Dr. Carritte, was called in to treat Esther's bizarre condition. Unfortunately, Dr. Carritte was little prepared for what he was about to face, and every time he tried to administer a sedative to Esther he was chased out of the room by flying objects. On one occasion, while investigating the basement, he was pelted by a shower of potatoes until he fled back up the stairs. It seemed that every time he tried to help poor Esther, he was met with the full fury of the poltergeist. Finally one evening, at his wits' end, he sank into a large chair to watch Esther rest when he heard a scratching sound on the wall behind him. Turning around, he stared in amazement as the words "Esther Cox, you are mine to kill" formed in the plaster as if carved by a sharp knife.

When word of the strange happenings leaked out, crowds of people began to gather at the Teed cottage and several times the police had to be called out to disperse the mob. Although the public was more than curious about what was happening to Esther Cox, they were certainly not sympathetic to her plight. Many thought that she just needed a good belt across the backside, while the church simply dismissed the matter as a result of newly commercialized electricity. Given both the attention and the hostility that Esther was receiving, Daniel Teed decided that she should stay at the house of a neighbor, John White, until things cooled down a bit. While she was away, things returned to normal in the Teed home, although Esther continued to experience attacks, many of which were witnessed by White.

When Esther returned home from her forced vacation, the poltergeist renewed its attacks with even greater ferocity. Small fires began igniting around the house and on one occasion witnesses watched as lighted matches appeared out of thin air and fell onto Esther's bed. In fact, the Amherst fire department was called to the Teed household so many times they began to suspect Esther of arson. The last straw came when a bucket of cedar shavings burst into flames in the basement, nearly burning down the cottage. The landlord made it perfectly clear by this point that "either Esther went or they all did."

Around this time, Walter Hubbell appeared. Hubbell was by trade a local actor and by nature a grand showman. He convinced the Teeds that if he could exhibit young Esther to the public and dazzle observers with the amazing phenomena that swirled around her, they would all be rich. The poltergeist, however, had other plans and when Esther took to the stage, the entity refused even to make a sound. Hubbell and Esther were booed off the stage and the audience members demanded their money back. Undaunted by the initial setback, Hubbell believed he could still make a buck and moved into the Teed cottage to study the entity for a book he proposed to write. The experience, however, would be a little more than he bargained for; he quickly learned, as had the doctor, that any attempts to help Esther only made him a target, too. During his stay, he was attacked with everything from his own umbrella to a carving knife that slammed into the wall just a few inches from his head.

There seemed no defense against an invisible enemy who day by day was becoming more violent. An attempted exorcism by the Reverend R. A. Temple only resulted in his being chased out by the blaring of invisible trumpets—after which, the poltergeist spent the rest of the night blowing trumpets in a bizarre victory celebration. Mr. Teed could stand no more and decided to throw Esther out of the house for the last time. She went to work at the nearby farm of Arthur Davison and his wife, where the Davisons and others witnessed numerous instances of continued hostility from the poltergeist. The activity reached a climax when the Davisons' barn burned to the ground. Esther was charged with arson and sentenced to four months in jail, although she was released after serving only one month. It seems that her imprisonment was enough to break the poltergeist's hold on her, for the incidents tapered off after that and eventually stopped.

The Amherst case is much like other poltergeist experiences in that the manifestations centered on one person or focus. The activity only occurred when Esther Cox was present in the home and, during the intervals that she was away, it ceased altogether. In fact, true to form, it even followed her to the White and Davison residences, where it continued to demonstrate its ability to manifest wherever she was present. But Esther was more than just the focus of the poltergeist; she was also its primary target. During the attacks, she displayed horrible physical symptoms including body swelling, bulging of the eyes, and hair that reportedly stood on end. She was stuck with pins on more than one occasion, and the entity literally spelled out its intention to kill her. While it's true that there were others who faced the entity's wrath, including Hubbell and the family doctor, it's important to note that they were largely ignored until they showed an interest in Esther. They only came under attack when they tried to help her or in some way interfered with the actions of the poltergeist.

But is there more to this story than a young woman being tormented by a random entity seemingly bent on her destruction? Esther Cox was living in an environment ripe with tension when the attacks began. The cottage that the Teeds lived in was too small for the extended family and, because of cramped living conditions, Esther was forced to share a bed with her sister Jennie. More importantly, however, Esther had narrowly avoided rape at the hands of a suitor just a week before the incidents began.

Even without the added trauma of experiencing an assault, puberty is a difficult and uncertain time for young people as new thoughts, feelings, and hormones rush through their system, changing the composition of both their body and brain. This causes a great deal of anxiety and turmoil as they struggle to cope with these changes. High levels of stress are found in many poltergeist cases and it is believed that psychological tension may act as a trigger for the manifestations. It is for this reason that scientists soon turned to the focus as the key to the poltergeist riddle, and theorized that the source of the phenomenon lay not in demons or ghosts, but in people themselves.

The theory that poltergeists are the result of what is termed "recurrent spontaneous psychokinesis" (RSPK) has gained wide support with researchers and scientists over the years. In a nutshell, it states that, as psychological tensions build within the focus, RSPK acts as a release valve, allowing the subconscious to act out in ways that the focus consciously cannot. The emotional energy created by the tension is converted into a supercharged force that can cause percussive sounds, move objects, and in short, cause most of the phenomena associated with poltergeist activity.

Many times the nature of this activity is self-punishing as young people struggle with the guilt and anxiety of powerful emotions, becoming the target of their own need to lash out. The focus is not aware that he or she is the source of the disturbance and, because RSPK releases negative tension, the focus often experiences a sense of relief after each poltergeist episode. In the case of Esther Cox, we find that immediately after the booming thunder and massive swelling subsided, she was able to fall right to sleep—behavior that may have surprised the rest of her family, who lay awake the remainder of the night, too frightened to close their eyes.

If we examine a more modern case known as the Enfield poltergeist, we find that it bears a close resemblance to the events in Amherst. Our story begins in Enfield, a suburb of London, England, at the home of Peggy Hodgson and her four children: Margaret (age 13); Janet (11); Pete (10); and Jimmy (7). It was an average home by English standards, sitting on a quiet street. That is, until the night of August 31, 1977, when Peggy heard a commotion coming from the room that Janet and Pete shared. When she entered their room, the children complained that they had heard shuffling noises, as if someone were walking across the floor in slippers. About to scold the children for making too much noise, Peggy stopped when she heard the sound herself, followed by four loud knocks against the wall. Then as if on cue, a large heavy chest moved several feet away from the wall by itself, but when she tried to push it back into place, it refused to budge. Fearing for her children, Peggy grabbed all four, still in their pajamas, and fled to a neighbor's house.

Gary Nottingham was a builder by trade and a man who didn't believe in such things as ghosts, but when the frightened Hodgson family showed up on his doorstep that night, he agreed to go next door and check things out. As he searched the house for what he thought might be a prowler, he also heard the knocking without finding its source. Instead, he opted to call the police and let them deal with it, but when they arrived, they too were dumbfounded by the knocking. While they continued to search the house, a chair slid several feet in their direction unassisted, but since they could find no laws being broken, there was little they could do.

Because the police were powerless to help, Peggy Hodgson called the *Daily Mirror*, which responded by sending several reporters and a photographer. While investigating the house, the reporters witnessed small toys flying about unassisted. One of these, a small Lego block, struck the photographer in the forehead hard enough to leave a bruise. However, as hard as they tried, they were unable to record any of the manifestations due to equipment that mysteriously malfunctioned at just the right time.

One week after the poltergeist began its playful romp, two investigators from the SPR, Maurice Grosse and Guy Lyon Playfair, arrived. Over the course of the next year they documented approximately two thousand examples of poltergeist manifestations, all of which seemed to center around eleven-year-old Janet. But to their frustration, Grosse and Playfair were plagued by the same types of equipment failures that the reporters had experienced. Just before a manifestation, camera batteries drained by themselves and, in some cases, parts in the recording devices were bent or destroyed within their protective casing.

As the manifestations progressed, they became more and more violent, reaching a destructive peak around December 15—a time that coincided with the beginning of Janet's menstrual cycle. Fires mysteriously sprang up around the home, smells of rotten cabbage permeated rooms, and obscene messages were found scribbled on walls. Worse yet, Janet began displaying signs similar to those of spirit possession such as drifting into trancelike states, twitching and convulsing, and growling in a deep voice. When researchers attempted to communicate with the entity through a series of coded raps, they learned that the poltergeist claimed to be not one, but several personalities, all of whom said that they were spirits of the dead. In one conversation, researchers were able to goad the entity into demonstrating its power by materializing a tea bag for them.

As with most poltergeist cases, as time went on the manifestations became less frequent until ceasing altogether by October 1978. As the incidents subsided, the children seemed almost reluctant to lose their newfound source of attention and on several occasions were caught faking manifestations. This does not, however, disqualify the Enfield poltergeist from being classified as legitimate poltergeist activity. In the majority of instances, neither natural explanations nor trickery can explain the manifestations that occurred in the Hodgson home during this period.

As in the Amherst case, the poltergeist appeared to center on a young girl who was experiencing stress and, in Janet's case, just beginning puberty. Some investigators believe that the stress in this case stemmed from unresolved feelings associated with Peggy's divorce from the children's father. In fact, when this possibility was suggested to Peggy, she began working to come to terms with this issue, at about the same time when the manifestations began to taper off. It's difficult to say whether the poltergeist disappeared because troubling issues within the family were resolved or because it had simply run its course. Researchers today, including William Roll and others, suggest the best exorcism for banishing pesky poltergeists is nothing more than obtaining counseling for the focuses and their families. If healthy outlets can be found for the focuses to express themselves, and the internal tensions within the family units are addressed, then the poltergeists will lose their power and fade away.

———•◦•———

But does modern science hold the key to the poltergeist question or are scientists as misguided as their earlier counterparts? After all, weren't the priests and mediums before them as confident with their answers as scientists are today? Over the centuries, the image of the poltergeist has changed from demon, to ghost, to the dark subconscious of man himself, but is there yet another answer to the poltergeist, something we haven't considered? In another century, will the poltergeist again exchange its mask for something new?

Chapter 8

GHOSTBUSTERS

There are mysteries which men can only guess at, which
age by age they may solve only in part.

— BRAM STOKER, *Dracula*

*O*n the 1984 hit movie *Ghostbusters*, Bill Murray, Dan Aykroyd, Harold Ramis, and Ernie Hudson donned bulky proton packs and raced off into the dark streets of New York City, hunting ghosts. Complete with their very own soundtrack and a wide array of cool gadgets topped with flashing lights, this comic foursome became a household name overnight. Whether it was free-floating, full-torso apparitions, focused non-terminal repeating phantasms, or even those nasty little slimers, no job was too big for the Ghostbusters. That, however, is the problem with movies—they usually fall short of real life, and the history of ghost hunting little resembles anything found on the big screen. Instead, actual ghost hunters spend long, tiresome hours doing research, conducting interviews, and trying to convince reluctant proprietors or homeowners to let them run around their property setting up equipment and snapping photos. Finally, when all the prep work is done, they get to sit in some damp cemetery or old house all night, hoping for just one tiny sound recording or indistinct picture of a ghost. Yet despite all of this, ghost hunting has attracted many gifted and adventurous men and women who have sacrificed time, money, and sometimes their very reputations for the pursuit.

So far in this book we've looked at some of the Spiritualists, churchmen, and scientists who have left their mark on the field of psychical research, but the professional ghost hunters that emerged in the twentieth century were altogether something different. As Spiritualism gained popular attention, most people quickly broke into two camps: those who believed in the phenomena and those who questioned its authenticity. From the beginning, the two sides took shots at one another in what would become a very exciting and profitable soap opera for the newspapers of the day. Each week some hot new medium came forward with the ability to perform fantastic wonders while skeptics railed against him or her with accusations of spiritual forgery. It was from this conflict that the modern ghost hunter emerged: neither churchman, medium, nor scientist, but a unique blend of all three.

The rest of this chapter is devoted to briefly recounting the tales of a few of the ghost hunters who have captured the public's imagination. Despite numerous scandals and controversies in the field (or perhaps because of them), ghost hunters continue to captivate us to this day, finding their way into books, movies, and an occasional news article around Halloween. By understanding their stories, we may come to understand just what it is they are looking for. In doing so, we may even catch a glimpse of ourselves. So without further ado, allow me to introduce to you . . .

The Mysterious Harry

*I expect the grim fiend is following me up in
these tricks, and he may catch me someday yet.*
—Harry Houdini

Harry Houdini stood under the stage lights, once again ready to face death before a packed house. After a few conjuring tricks to warm up the audience, he stripped down to a pair of trunks and announced to the expectant crowd that they were about to witness the most dangerous feat in the world: the infamous "Chinese water torture cell." To ensure that he was not concealing any keys or lock-picking tools, several audience members were invited onstage to search his body and examine the heavy cuffs and chains used to restrain him. Once tightly bound, his body was hoisted upside down above a glass cabinet of water. After a brief pause to allow the audience to soak in the drama, he was submerged headfirst into the cabinet, already struggling with his chains. The orchestra began an ominous tune as the tank was sealed and a curtain raised around it.

The audience moved closer to the edge of their seats, suffering each passing moment as if they were chained in the tank alongside Houdini, struggling for life. "How could any mortal man hold his breath for so long?" they asked one another. Or was this to be the end of "The Great and Mysterious Harry"? Houdini's assistants began shifting nervously as they stood with fire axes ready should anything go wrong and they needed to free him from his watery tomb. The tension was becoming too much and some of the more faint of heart in the audience began to pass out with fright. Then a great cheer of relief went up as Houdini burst from behind the curtain and the music changed to a triumphal march. He was exhausted and dripping wet, but in his hands he carried the chains that once bound him within the water tank. Once again he had escaped the jaws of death. It was a miracle—it was Harry Houdini.

Houdini was born Erich Weiss of Appleton, Wisconsin, in 1874, and later took the name Harry Houdini when he took to the stage. Houdini's parents were immigrants from Hungary who spoke little English and spent most of their lives in dire poverty. While still a young boy, Houdini's father abandoned the family and Harry was forced to find work with the rest of his brothers to help put food on the table. Times were tough for the Weiss family, and although Houdini worked hard each day, he still managed to visit as many carnival sideshows, traveling showmen, and curiosity shops as possible developing an obsession for magic tricks, feats of illusion, and other strange performances.

It was during these early years that Harry encountered his first medium. It seems that he and a friend wrangled an invitation to a séance with a medium named Minnie Williams, a rather robust woman specializing in spirit materialization. Eager to witness spirits of the dead imparting wisdom from the other world, Harry was instead treated to his first lesson in fraudulent mediumship. Williams's daughter collected one dollar from each of the forty guests, the lights dimmed, and the show began. For most of the guests, ghosts appeared to roam about the room, speaking in otherworldly voices, but to young Harry's careful eye there were serious problems with the performance.

For instance, as the ghosts materialized, he noticed the floorboards creaking under their weight as they "floated" by, suggesting they were not as light or as ethereal as they pretended to be. Also, as each ghost paraded before the stunned audience, whether it was meant to be a young babe or an old hag, its appearance changed very little. In fact, they all looked the same—more closely resembling the large figure of the medium wrapped in a shroud than anything else. The worst was yet to come, however; as the spirits uttered their ghostly pronouncements throughout the séance, Harry thought that each ghost sounded curiously like the muffled voice of Williams. (Either that or all the spirits happened to have a head cold that day.)

If Houdini wasn't impressed by the séance, then later on he certainly proved that he could do better. In 1897, he and his wife Bess joined Dr. Hill's California Concert Company, performing mind reading tricks and faking spirit communications. The two were an instant draw, and Houdini often got the crowd going with a few escape tricks or other illusions before he moved on to reading the contents of sealed letters or raising a few ghosts. The act, however, was short-lived and Houdini later related that it was canceled because of several strange incidents that unsettled him deeply. Houdini believed that he had received a form of second sight from his mother and, during one mind reading act, he felt he had discovered the true identity of a murderer. To Houdini, there was something more than just parlor tricks to all this—sometimes it was real. After this he steered clear of the séance room and stuck to the escape routines that would make him famous.

It wasn't until the guns of World War I sounded that Houdini again took an interest in Spiritualism. As thousands of young men failed to return from the slaughter of the war, loved ones increasingly turned to Spiritualism to help them cope with their loss. Houdini watched with mounting frustration as spiritual charlatans preyed upon distraught parents and grieving widows. The issue soon struck closer to home for Houdini when his own beloved mother died while he was traveling Europe in 1913. Convinced that she had an important message to give to him on her deathbed, Houdini tried desperately to contact her spirit. Disappointingly, in séance after séance he found not proof of his mother's spiritual existence but cheap magic tricks designed to make a quick buck. The world, it seemed, was still full of frauds like Minnie Williams, stumbling around in the dark pretending to be ghosts.

It was at this point that Houdini began to investigate mediums in earnest, often entering a séance disguised as an old man with a fake beard and spectacles. When the séance reached its peak and Houdini was sure of the medium's deception, he would jump to his feet and, shining a flashlight on the stunned medium, confront him or her with the fraud. Afterward, news reporters hungry for a scoop waited outside, ready to record the latest skirmish between Houdini and the Spiritualists. The papers loved the drama and Houdini was far from averse to putting on a good show. Needless to say, his popularity with members of the Spiritualist movement was never good, and at best they came to see him as an uncomfortable thorn in their side.

One of Houdini's most controversial exposures involved the Boston medium Mina Crandon, or Margery as she liked to be called. In 1922, the publisher of *Scientific American* magazine offered twenty-five hundred dollars (later doubled), to any person capable of producing genuine psychic phenomena before a committee of judges. At first no one took the bait and the publisher began to worry that the challenge would go unanswered. Finally Dr. LeRoi Crandon stepped forward and requested that the committee investigate his wife Margery, who was becoming something of a sensation for her ability to produce an ectoplasmic hand that could manipulate objects.

Houdini, who was a member of the committee, was sure that she was nothing more than a clever fraud, even if the rest of the judges were impressed with her ability. To test her powers, he had a wooden box specially designed to allow only her head and arms to stick out when she was seated within it. Once in the box, she was asked to command her spirit guide, Walter (her deceased brother), to ring a bell several feet away as a sign of his presence. After several lengthy attempts, however, she was unable to manifest any sort of spirit activity, much less ring a bell. Frustrated with the tight controls, Margery's spirit guide lashed out, claiming that Houdini had secreted a ruler in the box in order to discredit her. A careful search was made and indeed a collapsible ruler was found hidden within the box. In turn, Houdini struck back with his own accusations, claiming Margery planned to use the ruler to move objects with her mouth while leaving her hands free during the séance. Regardless of who was responsible for the ruler, enough doubt was cast on the proceedings that neither Margery nor anyone else was able to claim the prize. In the end, no one came forward who could prove a mediumistic ability and so the prize was withdrawn.

On October 24, 1926, the man who had beaten death time and again gave his last performance in Detroit, Michigan, before being rushed to Grace Hospital with a ruptured appendix. After several operations, Houdini lingered for a few more days before dying in his wife's arms on October 31—Halloween. Ironically, the man who came to be known as the scourge of Spiritualism also became its victim, as reports began flooding in from all over the globe from mediums claiming that Houdini had reached out to them with a message from the Great Beyond.

In his lifetime, Harry Houdini was considered by his detractors as the worst of skeptics with an ironclad inability to believe. But the truth is that he was a believer and that more than a desire for press clippings drove him in his search for proof of an afterlife. He was an illusionist and conjurer who saw through the cleverest tricks of his contemporaries, and his exposure of the widespread deceit practiced by mediums did much to advance the field of psychic research. Although he spent much of his life facing death, he never did find the ghosts he was looking for. Mediums to this day claim that Houdini still pops up in séances on Halloween night, the anniversary of his death. And who knows? He was, after all, "The Mysterious Harry."

THE GREATEST
GHOST HUNTER IN ALL OF ENGLAND

If any entity is present here tonight,
will it please make itself known.
— HARRY PRICE

It all began one cold and moonless night in an old English manor, much as any good ghost story does. The clock showed that it was almost midnight when fifteen-year-old Harry Price heard the sounds of stomping on the floors above him, a sound that echoed through the manor's dark halls and filled the room in which he and a friend were hiding.

The village folk had warned the boys that for many a long year spirits had roamed the old place. It was said that the manor was once owned by a man who went crazy and strangled his beautiful young niece before taking his own life. Since then, queer things had been happening at the old manor, and its most recent owners had deserted the place, telling of wispy forms and strange noises in the night. Nevertheless, Harry Price wasn't the type of boy to be turned away by such stories; in fact, they were what had lured him to the house in the first place. After obtaining permission to spend the night in the manor, he and a friend set a camera at the landing of the main staircase where legend told of a spirit that climbed its steps at night. The two boys then ran a cord from the camera to a locked room where they would be sleeping and settled back in quiet anticipation.

Their waiting was over as the sounds moved from one room to another on the floors above. Finally, the stomping made its way to the staircase, which creaked as someone or something slowly descended. When the footsteps reached the very last step, the sounds stopped entirely. Sensing that the ghost was now in full view of the camera lens, Harry pulled the cord to activate the camera. A brilliant flash of light pierced the seal of the room's door, followed by a terrific explosion that startled the boys. When they recovered enough nerve to open the door and cautiously peek their heads out, they found the stairs' landing wrapped in a thick blanket of smoke that sent both boys into fits of coughing. When the air cleared, the two ventured out and picked up their overturned camera. There was no evidence of any ghost, only the lingering smell of flash powder. It seems young Harry had used too much powder in the camera's flash pan, which, when triggered, resulted in an explosion that shook the room and upset the camera. Later, when the boys developed the plate, they were disappointed to find only an overdeveloped picture of an empty staircase. Although Harry Price was unable to catch evidence of any wandering spirits that night, he did begin a lifelong obsession with ghosts that promised many strange adventures. With that first blinding flash of the camera, a ghost hunter was born. Not just any ghost hunter, as time would prove, but the greatest ghost hunter in all of England.

Harry Price was born in London on January 17, 1881. Little is known of his childhood other than what he related himself. We do know that Price was not above stretching the truth to fit the story he wanted to tell. For instance, Price repeatedly claimed to have been born into an affluent family in Shropshire, with his father the owner of a paper-making firm. The truth of the matter is that Price's origins were a bit humbler; his father was actually a grocer and later a traveling salesman. Erroneous claims such as these were used after his death by his detractors to question the credibility not only of his character, but of his work as well.

We know that, after finishing school, Price drifted from one job to another, never quite feeling comfortable with the roles he chose to play. The one constant thing in his life seemed to be his love for the illusion of magic, which later earned him the title of master conjurer. But like that night in the manor, fate would favor him with a flash and a bang. In 1908, while working as a journalist, he met and married the wealthy heiress Constance Mary Knight. Suddenly Harry was a man of wealth. Some men would have sat back, content to enjoy their new life of leisure, but for Harry there would always be that old haunted manor calling to him. For him, a haunted house remained more than just a place of dusty corridors and cobwebbed doorways. It was a place of dark enchantment where secrets waited to be revealed; it was the ultimate magic trick.

Price decided to turn both his attention and newfound wealth toward investigating ghosts. In 1920, he joined the SPR and, with his extensive knowledge of magic and illusion, he was soon considered a leading expert at debunking fraudulent mediums. The most famous of these was the "spirit" photographer William Hope, whom Price caught double-exposing pictures and claiming the fuzzy extras were spirits of the dead. But in direct contrast to his American counterpart, Harry Houdini, Harry Price also publicly endorsed a number of mediums that he thought were genuine. These included Stella Cranshaw in 1923 and Rudi Schneider in 1929, on both of whom he staked considerable time, money, and reputation. Such a gamble, though popular with the press, caused a rift between Price and fellow investigators in the SPR who were devoutly opposed to Spiritualism. Undaunted by this, he decided he needed greater freedom in his research and so broke with the SPR, creating in 1934 the National Laboratory of Psychical Research, which today is part of the University of London.

For Price, apparently the only thing better than being behind the camera photographing ghosts was being in front of it. Always the publicity seeker, he attempted several stunts that failed miserably, from investigating an invisible talking mongoose named Gef to sleeping in a haunted bed. His biggest fiasco, however, occurred in 1932, when he led an expedition into Germany's Harz Mountains. There, on the tallest peak, he attempted a fifteenth-century magical ritual from the *Bloksberg Tryst*, the "High German Black Book," which promised to turn a simple farm goat into a handsome young man.

The ritual began with a large magic circle accompanied by ancient symbols drawn in the ground. Then a pure young maiden led a white goat into the circle and covered it with a sheet. Harry, acting as the high priest in the matter, burned incense and mixed unguents of bats' blood, church bell scrapings, soot, and honey while chanting Latin incantations. When the last magical syllable was uttered and the ritual ended, a large group of reporters crowded around the sheet with cameras ready. Needless to say, when Price lifted the sheet, there was no newly transformed lad underneath, only a frightened goat. The ceremony had failed and, whether Price was just having a bit of fun or was trying to get attention, the press continued to take shots at him for some time, even dubbing him "the Goat Man." Regardless of these setbacks, Price continued with dogged persistence writing, lecturing, and investigating claims of the supernatural. His investigations of Borley Rectory, his most famous case, are considered groundbreaking in the field of paranormal research.

Borley Rectory in Essex—later popularized by Price as "the most haunted house in all of England"—was a massive red brick building dating to 1863. Residents had reported strange happenings since shortly after it was built, and locals claimed it stood atop numerous other structures far more ancient. In 1929, Price was asked by the editor of the London *Daily Mirror* to investigate the many claims of hauntings. One of the most persistent tales recounted was that a beautiful young novice from a Catholic convent had secretly fallen in love with the convent's coachman and the two decided to elope. The young lovers were betrayed, however, and once caught, they were brought before their superiors. Their punishment was severe—the coachman was sentenced to be executed by the hangman's noose and the young woman was walled up alive in the convent. Since then, residents of the area reported a spectral nun walking the grounds of Borley, as well as a phantom coach, complete with a team of horses, that rushes up to the front of the house and then disappears. To further the mystery of the place, several rectors had died while living there and they too were thought to roam the building.

For the most part Borley was a quiet, old haunted house until poltergeist-like activity began in 1930, immediately after the Reverend Lionel Foyster and his wife Marianne moved in. Strange activity seemed to occur whenever Marianne was present. Rocks were hurled at the rectory, objects moved or were smashed by unseen hands, and dark figures were seen flitting from room to room. The most bizarre manifestations, though, were small childlike writings that appeared on the walls when no one was present, addressing Marianne by name, as well as scraps of parchment paper that were found lying around with words such as "light," "mass," and "prayers" written in the same small handwriting. The Reverend Foyster began keeping a diary of these almost daily occurrences and Borley began to receive a lot of attention by both curiosity seekers and the press.

After five years of this, the Foysters finally decided that they could stand it no longer and left the rectory, giving its empty rooms and corridors back to the ghosts that haunted them. From the beginning, Price suspected that Marianne was the real source behind much of the phenomena. Many of the manifestations seemed either to occur only when she was present or were tied to her in other ways. This led Price to believe that perhaps she had faked some of the reported events in order to draw attention to herself. After all, hadn't the ghostly behavior of Borley's spirits catapulted her from the obscurity of being a country reverend's wife to tabloid stardom? In spite of this, Price still felt there were things taking place at Borley that could not be explained as naturally occurring phenomena or human trickery. When Borley was offered for rent in 1937, Price saw the opportunity of a lifetime: his very own haunted house. He quickly leased the property for one year and assembled a team of about forty investigators who lived night and day at the rectory, hoping to record evidence of its ghostly inhabitants.

During the course of the investigation, researchers recorded countless manifestations involving unexplained lights, cold spots, apparitions, and cryptic writing that appeared on the walls. After one revealing séance, the remains of a woman were discovered in the cellar, which Price thought added credibility to the legend of the phantom nun. Her bones were later given a proper burial in consecrated ground in the hope that her ghost would find peace. As if in response to this puzzle, several religious medals of Catholic origin appeared out of nowhere at the rectory and the phantom nun was never seen again.

To date, Borley Rectory remains one of the most intensely studied haunted houses in history and Price went on to write several popular books about his investigations there, adding to his own fame and that of the rectory. Shortly after Price and his team concluded their study, tragedy struck the rectory for the last time. In 1939, while new tenants were moving in, a carelessly placed oil lamp spilled, causing a fire that consumed the building, leaving only a brick shell that was later demolished. The "most haunted house in England" was no more. With its destruction, Price moved on to other investigations, but none would ever match the fame of Borley Rectory.

In 1948, Harry Price died of a heart attack at his home in West Sussex. A man of strong and often public opinion, Price made many enemies during his life as he wavered between the Spiritualist and scientific communities. He was known to guard his discoveries with almost parental jealousy, whether it was a promising new medium or a haunted house. It was for reasons such as these that he was so easily attacked after his death with charges ranging from embellishing the details of investigations to outright fraud.

Regardless of the charges leveled against him, Harry Price was undoubtedly a tireless investigator. Through his National Laboratory, he lectured on psychic research, invented devices to test mediums, and studied everything from fire walking to Hindu rope tricks. His greatest contribution to the field will always be his investigation of Borley Rectory, which continues to inspire debate among researchers and to draw curiosity seekers to the site. To this day, there are those who claim that ghost lights appear where the rectory once stood and that spirits of the dead still walk its grounds. Harry Price spent his life chasing the mysteries that others would not dare to risk their reputation on. For all his triumphs and failures, what continued to drive him was the pure wonder and excitement of it all. For Harry Price, it was always about a young boy in a haunted house looking for ghosts.

THE DEMONOLOGISTS

I've never met an atheist in a haunted house.
— ED WARREN

Ed and Lorraine Warren stood on the snow-covered lawn waiting for the rest of their research team to arrive. Before them towered a rambling Dutch colonial home that grew darker as the sun set over the township of Amityville, Long Island. The house had recently made headlines when its latest owners, George and Kathy Lutz, fled with their family in fear one night after having lived in the house for only twenty-eight days. They claimed that hooded apparitions, swarms of flies, sickening smells, and an invisible marching band that nightly paraded through their living room had terrorized them. They were so frightened by what was happening around them that they simply abandoned their new home, leaving with only the clothes on their backs. Later they refused to enter the house for any reason, even to collect the furniture and other belongings they left behind.

But the house that quietly stared back at the Warrens was no stranger to sinister headlines. Just one year before the Lutz family purchased the place, it had been the site of a grisly mass murder. On November 13, 1974, twenty-three-year-old Ronald DeFeo Jr. slaughtered his parents and four younger siblings while they slept. During his subsequent trial, the prosecution maintained that Ronnie's motivation was a two-hundred-thousand-dollar life insurance policy and a large sum of cash in the family safe. DeFeo, however, shocked the jury when he told them that what led him to kill his entire family was not the desire for material gain, but a host of demonic voices that filled his head, urging him to kill.

The house seemed a magnet for suffering and darkness and tales linking it to past tragedies were rampant. It was said to occupy an area where the Shinnecock tribe of Native Americans had once housed their sick and insane. In addition, rumors that a former owner had practiced black magic on the property only added to its reputation. Now, for the first time since the Lutz family abandoned it that terrible night, someone was daring to enter it again. Although the Warrens were experienced ghost hunters who had been involved in psychical research for years, they had no idea of the evil that waited for them within.

Ed and Lorraine Warren grew up on opposite sides of the tracks in Bridgeport, Connecticut. Ed, born in 1926, came from a tough section of town known as "the Bloody Bucket" and until the age of twelve lived in a house he maintains was haunted. It was here that Ed received his first brush with the spirit world. As a child he experienced unexplained pounding, raps, and footsteps, and often saw the apparition of an old woman who peered out at him from his closet at night. His father, however, was a pragmatic man and a police officer that found little room in his daily life for "children's spooks." Although he could never fully explain the bizarre events occurring in their home, neither would he admit they were the work of spiritual agents. Ed learned early the lesson that skepticism can be as blind as faith.

Lorraine Rita Moran, born in 1927, attended Laurelton Hall, a private school in Milford, Connecticut, where as a young girl she discovered that she had rather unusual gifts. While she was at school, she began to notice a glow surrounding people. As unique as a fingerprint, these auras changed in size, shape, and color depending on the mood and personality of a person. As she grew older, the auras became more distinct and other abilities began to surface, including clairvoyance and trance mediumship—tools that would later serve her well as a professional ghost hunter.

The two met as teenagers at the local movie house and eventually married in 1945. After serving in World War II, Ed attended art school and enjoyed painting landscapes and nautical scenes, but his greatest passion was painting houses reputed to be haunted. The young couple would drive through the New England countryside in their old Chevy, looking for haunted houses to paint. While Ed busied himself with his brushes and canvas, Lorraine chatted with the owners, pumping them for whatever stories they could provide. Soon the two found they were spending less time with the canvas and more time inside the houses. With Ed's growing knowledge of the occult and Lorraine's developing psychic ability, it wasn't long before the couple devoted themselves entirely to investigating. This led to the formation of the New England Society for Psychical Research (NESPR) in 1952; its goal remains to investigate claims of the supernatural while educating the public about the world of spirits and demons. Ed and Lorraine were now officially ghost hunters.

Back at the house in Amityville, Lorraine took one stair at a time, allowing her senses to spread out before her like psychic radar, searching for impressions. The rest of the team was spread out over the first floor, setting up their equipment, but it was the second floor that Lorraine was concerned with—after all, that was where the murders had taken place and the impressions there should be the strongest. The house bothered her and, even before she had agreed to come here, she had called friends in the clergy and asked them to pray for the investigators' safety. As she slowly climbed the grand staircase, she listened to her senses, clutching a relic from Padre Pio, the Italian saint, for protection. Suddenly she braced herself. Something was coming down the stairs toward her; she could feel it—something angry, something evil. An invisible force slammed against her like a tidal wave of rushing water and, with each step she took, the atmosphere grew thicker as if the air were solidifying. She knew what it wanted. It wanted her to turn back.

Lorraine pressed on, and upon reaching the second floor, the invisible force suddenly stopped. Shaken, she knew she had to continue because it was here, in the rooms of the second floor, that the DeFeo family had been brutally murdered by one of their own. The first room that she entered was a child's room, most recently belonging to Missy Lutz. Immediately it struck her, as she stared at the small, colorful children's furniture, that many of the items in the rooms had belonged to the murdered DeFeo girls. It seemed that when the Lutzes purchased the house, much of the furniture came with it. The new family had even slept in the beds in which the DeFeo children had died. From room to room she explored with her psychic senses telling her the same thing—everything was saturated with horror.

While Lorraine and the rest of the team searched the house, Ed made his way down the cellar steps. If there was anything haunting this house, it would be focused down there, he reasoned. It was in the cellar that the Lutz family reported overwhelming smells of dried blood; it was also where a secret room, painted red, was discovered under the stairwell. It was rare for Ed to pick up psychic impressions—that was his wife's talent—but something was drawing him to the cellar. At the bottom of the stairs, the cellar stretched out in both directions. One side led to a paneled room the children used as a playroom, while the other contained a massive boiler. It was then that Ed began to notice that the shadows cast by the overhead lights were actually moving and changing forms. A pinpoint of light appeared and hovered in the air over his head—then another and another, until there seemed to be thousands clustering in the shadows. Drawing closer, the serpentine shadows began to press around him. He felt weight and form behind their slippery movements, as if they wanted to drag him to the ground. Ed knew he was in great danger. These were no mere ghosts. This was pure evil. Ed steadied himself, resisting their pressure. He began to pray aloud, casting holy water at their movements and commanding them to leave in the name of Jesus Christ. The shadows swirled around him angrily as he felt the sickening sensation of something trying to lift him from the ground.

When the group assembled again on the first floor, Ed seemed visibly shaken. His struggle with the dark entities in the cellar had sapped his strength. Lorraine looked uneasy, too. The impressions of suffering and horror were all around them. The house was beginning to take its toll on the others as well and several in the group started to feel unwell. One member even had to be taken outside for fresh air and then refused to enter the house again. Watching the house affect the others caused Ed and Lorraine to worry. The evil of the place was working on each of them, wearing them down. It was one a.m. when the Warrens and their team left the house. They were exhausted by the experience and some present that night would claim health problems for months to come.

The Lutz family went on to sell their story to author Jay Anson, who dramatized the events in the 1977 bestseller *The Amityville Horror*. A movie followed in 1979 and soon people were flocking to theatres to be scared by the story. The house at 112 Ocean Avenue in Amityville, Long Island, became a household name across America and gawkers descended upon the formerly quiet town.

Immediately after the story broke, a storm of controversy rained down on both the Lutz family and the Warrens. Lawsuits flew back and forth and Lutz family members changed their story many times. The most damaging accusation came from DeFeo's defense attorney, William Weber, who in 1979 confessed that the story of the Amityville Horror was a hoax concocted by himself and George Lutz to make money; Weber also said that he hoped the publicity would help him to obtain a new trial for his client. Other researchers, most notably Dr. Stephen Kaplan, director of the Parapsychology Institute of America, found glaring discrepancies in the claims the Lutz family made. Kaplan stated, "After several months of extensive research and interviews with those who were involved in 'The Amityville Horror' . . . we found no evidence to support the claim of a 'haunted house.' What we did find is a couple that had purchased a house that they economically could not afford. It is our professional opinion that the story of its haunting is mostly fiction" (Harris 1986, 12).

Through all of this the Warrens neither confirmed nor denied the Lutz family's story, but they knew the house, felt the horrors within it, and continue to this day to stick by what they claimed happened in the house that night. Despite the fact that the haunting in Amityville is considered one of the greatest and most profitable hoaxes in history, the Warrens stood by their conviction that something evil lurked within the house.

Ed Warren passed away in 2006, but the work of the NESPR continues under Director Tony Spera, the Warrens' son-in-law. Lorraine Warren remains among the most sought-after lecturers in the paranormal field. Numerous books and movies have appeared chronicling the Warrens' adventures, and for a small fee you can tour a museum in their home filled with items from their encounters with the spirit realm. Whether or not Amityville is or ever really was haunted, Ed and Lorraine Warren were two of the most celebrated ghost hunters in America.

INTERVIEW WITH A GHOST HUNTER

Ghosts are real and they are everywhere.
— DAVE OESTER

Dave Oester and his wife Sharon Gill are founders of one of the largest ghost hunting organizations in the world, The International Ghost Hunters Society (IGHS). The IGHS is dedicated to the research and documentation of ghosts and apparitions through photography. Since first having become interested in ghost hunting in the 1990s, Dave and Sharon have appeared in countless newspaper articles, television programs, talk shows, and magazines, sharing with the public their love for ghost hunting. In the following interview, Dave was kind enough to take time from his busy schedule to share with us some of the knowledge and experience he has acquired over the years while ghost hunting.

Q: *In 1990, you became interested in the paranormal when you moved into a haunted house in Seaside, Oregon. Can you tell us more about this experience?*

A: The spirits that haunted the seaside cottage on Twelfth Street were playful spirits. I never had any serious negative issues with those spirits. The most common prank they pulled was to take an object, be it a book or something else, and not return it for several days. One prank that I remember was when I inserted new air filters into the oil furnace and a day later they vanished completely. They reappeared three days later, lying on top of the oil furnace ducting, where they would have been before they were removed. A young female spirit responded one time from the basement as I called down to my daughter. I decided not to disturb her and walked directly to the computer room where [my daughter] was playing on the computer.

Q: *How did these events affect you?*

A: It was the experiences of living in a haunted house that motivated me to begin collecting ghost stories from local people, and this led to writing the first book, *Twilight Visitors*, which had the story of the Twelfth Street house.

Q: *Is the house in Seaside still haunted?*

A: The house on Twelfth Street is still haunted today. The next family who moved into the house after we moved inland reported similar pranks that continued during their stay in the cottage.

Q: *Can you tell us a little bit about the IGHS and why it was founded?*

A: We posted our first ghost photos on our Web site, www .ghostweb.com, in July of 1996. At that time, there were maybe one or two Web sites about ghosts that received less than a thousand hits a year. In our first month we got over two thousand hits and we knew people were interested in what we were doing. We started getting swamped with e-mails asking if we offered a club that they could join. So in November of 1996, we started the International Ghost Hunters Society to help people learn how to photograph ghosts. The society expanded to include anyone who was a ghost believer, ghost hunter, or ghost researcher. The society has more than fourteen thousand members in eighty-seven countries. We started out with free membership and still offer free membership today. Our Web site is one of the largest and most popular ghost hunting Web sites on the Internet today. We get about three thousand e-mails a month from all over the world. Some are asking for help with hauntings; others want expert advice on their photographs.

Q: *What does the IGHS think ghosts really are?*

A: We have been teaching, since 1996, that ghosts are the essence of who people were in life, retaining intelligence, emotions, and personalities. Ghosts are people without physical bodies. Ghosts are not cursed to roam the earth, but some are anchored here because of unresolved issues, unfinished business, or because they simply want to remain here. Ghosts can come and go at will.

Q: *What are some of your favorite haunted sites?*

A: We love the haunts of New Mexico because the Indians were living in this land twelve thousand years ago. Their pueblos and great houses still have the spirits of those that lived a thousand years ago. The great kivas are excellent, as well as the old missions and forts. The Spanish conquistadors came in 1540 and so many sites are more than four hundred and sixty years old.

Q: *Do you use psychics during your investigations?*

A: No, we have not found that psychics were helpful. We found that if we had three separate psychics, we could get three separate explanations of what was happening. So many are claiming to be psychic, yet we find very little evidence that supports what they claim. We believe that everyone is sensitive to one degree or another and that each should work at developing their own skills, not listening to someone else for guidance.

Q: *What are some of the dangers involved in ghost hunting?*

A: Ghosts have knocked down people who have angered them by their rude and disrespectful attitudes. Ghosts are people without physical bodies, but they can get angry and upset at bad behavior, just as you and I. People who treat ghosts with respect will have no problems. Drinking and ghost hunting is a no-no. Alcohol has no place in an investigation. Those who are negative also have no place in an investigation. We are not here to prove anything to skeptics—let them find their own way in the dark. Ghosts avoid skeptics, just as I avoid them myself.

Q: *Tell us about one of the scariest encounters that you have had while hunting ghosts.*

A: The scariest moment for me was when I was investigating a cemetery by moonlight and accidentally stepped into soft dirt and my shoe sunk down into the loose dirt. I allowed my imagination to run wild, thought of all those television monster shows, and screamed. My scream scared Sharon, who screamed, and I screamed again hearing her scream. My heart was pumping like mad as I realized I had just sunk into the dirt a few inches; no hand had grabbed me and was pulling me into the grave.

Q: Is there anything that can be done to end a haunting, such as an exorcism?

A: No, the living have no control over the dead. Religious exorcisms do not work and generally cause more problems. We have never encountered demons or demonic creatures, nor have we ever found a valid case of possession; most who claim possession are looking for attention or have serious mental health issues. What people call "evil" or "demonic" is just a label to describe something they do not understand that scares them.

Q: How can a person interested in ghost hunting get started?

A: This is the easy part; anyone can be a ghost hunter. All it takes is a camera or tape recorder and, by following our simple standards and protocols, they can be successful. We offer free membership in the IGHS, we answer all e-mails sent to us without charge, and we never charge for investigations. We teach people how to investigate their own homes, not calling on someone else who may or may not be qualified. We have posted articles about how to begin ghost hunting and have hundreds of EVP ghost voices and thousands of photos [on our Web site] to examine.

Q: Any final advice for would-be ghost hunters?

A: Next time, imagine that the ghost is your late grandmother who is visiting her grandson or granddaughter. She is not demonic, but she is a family member on the other side of the grave who still loves her family members. If you loved her in life, why be afraid of her in death? Ghost hunting is a way to document the existence of life after death, proof of the survival of the soul. We can learn much from the spirits of the dead; after all, one day we will join them in their realm.

Chapter 9

GHOST HUNTING
101

There was wild work ahead of him tonight—enough wild work to last a lifetime.

— STEPHEN KING, *Pet Sematary*

When the editor of the *Daily Mirror* telephoned Harry Price in June 1929 and asked him to investigate the strange occurrences at Borley Rectory, Price wrote that he immediately began to stuff the following items into a large suitcase:

A pair of soft felt overshoes used for creeping, unheard, about the house in order that neither human beings nor paranormal "entities" shall be disturbed when producing "phenomena"; steel measuring tape for measuring rooms, passages, testing the thickness of walls in looking for secret chambers or hidey-holes; steel screw-eyes, lead post-office seals, sealing tool, strong cord or tape, and adhesive surgical tape for sealing doors, windows or cupboards; a set of tools with wire, nails, etc; hank of electric flex, small electric bells, dry batteries and switches (for secret electrical contacts); 9 cm. x 12 cm. Reflex camera, film packs, and flash-bulbs for indoor or outdoor photography; a small portable telephone for communicating with an assistant in another part of building or garden; notebook, red, blue, and black pencils; sketching block and case of drawing instruments for making plans; bandages, iodine and a flask of brandy in case a member of investigating staff or resident is injured or faints; ball of string, stick of chalk, matches, electric torch and candle;

bowl of mercury for detecting tremors in room or passage or for making silent electrical mercury switches;
cinematograph camera with remote electrical control,
and films; a sensitive transmitting thermograph, with
charts, to measure the slightest variation in temperature
in supposed haunted rooms; a packet of graphite and
soft brush for developing finger prints. For a long stay
in a house with supply of electricity, I would take with
me infra-red filters, lamps, and cine films sensitive to infra-red rays, so that I could take photographs in almost
complete darkness (Price 1990, 5–6).

Obviously Price wasn't a light packer when he traveled,
but the passage does illustrate the wide array of equipment
used by early ghost hunters. Since that time, improvements
in technology and research techniques have led to better-
informed and better-armed ghost hunters. Understanding
just how a modern investigation is conducted and the types
of equipment available is important to anyone who finds
him- or herself bitten by the ghost hunting bug. This chapter is by no means meant to limit first-time ghost hunters
to a series of hard and fast rules. Rather, think of this as a
set of guidelines pointing you in the right direction. Some
of the information you may find useful in conducting your
own investigation and some of it you may just choose to
disregard. The key is to remain flexible and creative in your
approach to ghost hunting and, above all, have fun and be
safe.

From churches to schoolhouses, hospitals to hotels, ghosts
have a tendency to pop up anywhere people once lived,
worked, or died. Therefore, in order to avoid the mistake of

assuming that every cemetery in town is haunted (and most really aren't), the first step that any ghost hunter must take is to know where to start looking. Just about every town or city is rich in its own brand of ghost lore and, thanks to the fact that we now live in an age of information, finding places reputed to be haunted is easier than ever.

Nowadays ghost hunters are coming to rely more and more on computers to help them during investigations, and a quick search on the Internet will bring up hundreds of Web sites devoted to ghost hunting. Some provide lists of places thought to be haunted (organized by region, state, or city), which can make it easier to find these locations in your area. In addition, ghost hunting clubs often have their own Web sites that provide information about their organization and what they do. Groups such as these are an excellent way to meet others interested in ghosts, learn practical investigative skills, and even join a ghost hunt or two.

Libraries are also wonderful places to find books and articles on haunted spots. Haunted directories and guidebooks can be found at many libraries and contain detailed histories of some of the more famous hauntings by writers who have spent considerable time researching the topic. If you can't find what you're looking for, don't be afraid to ask a librarian for help; it's what they get paid to do. Usually librarians are very knowledgeable when it comes to tracking down information and if for some reason they don't have what you need, they probably know how to get it. Better still, libraries contain reams of old news articles from local papers on microfilm and microfiche. Each year, as Halloween draws closer, reporters begin writing articles about local ghost lore and sites rumored to be haunted. Browsing old articles written each October can uncover a gold mine of spooky history in your area.

Another avenue to consider can't be found on a Web site or bookshelf, but in the oral histories of neighbors and family. Many times, people who have lived in an area for a period of time will be acquainted with those who have lived and died around them and may know if there are any local legends of worth. Knowledge of the surrounding area can provide leads unheard-of in most ghost books and Web sites. Some ghost hunters even place ads in the paper, asking anyone with information on haunted spots in their area to contact them and share their story. Be aware, however, that you'll have to sift through countless responses filled with urban legends and/or from attention-seeking kooks before you find anything useful. One important rule to consider is to always, regardless of the source, question the reliability of the information you receive—and this goes double for stories collected through a newspaper ad.

Once you've done the initial footwork and discovered a few promising leads, you'll need to decide what equipment to take with you. Since the time Harry Price first stuffed a suitcase full of everything but the kitchen sink, ghost hunters have come to use a wide array of devices to help them track down spirits. Becoming acquainted with the different types of equipment and how best to use them is important to the success of any investigation. A few dry runs should iron out any kinks and make it easier for you to use your equipment at night when visibility is poor. The following list includes those items most commonly used by ghost hunters today.

TOOLS OF THE TRADE

- A notebook and pens for recording field notes, making diagrams, and sketching maps of the location.

- A tape measure for determining distances.

- Several pieces of chalk to outline objects in order to determine if they have been moved.

- A small first-aid kit for emergencies.

- At least one cell phone in order to maintain contact with the outside world in case you need to call for help (or a pizza).

- Small tool kit for repairing equipment that breaks down in the field.

- Flashlights for each team member. These should be lightweight, durable, and waterproof. Red lenses work well because the light they produce is not as harsh as a clear lens. This will help reduce glare when trying to take notes or read instruments at night, and doesn't impair your night vision.

- Bring along a few glow sticks to serve as an alternative light source should your flashlights malfunction. Candles, kerosene lamps, and other flammables are never a good idea and run the risk of starting a fire.

Remember, even the famous Borley Rectory was consumed by one misplaced oil lamp.

- Two-way radios will help team members stay in contact with one another, as well as allowing you to coordinate team functions and movements. Headsets work particularly well and keep hands free for other things.

- A few well-placed infrared motion detectors can help secure an area and, when combined with a camera, can produce great results. However, they can be tricky to use and, if not careful, you'll have your own teams stumbling into them and setting them off.

- Electromagnetic field (EMF) detectors are very popular in ghost hunting today. Their use is based on the principle that spirits of the dead cause a disturbance in the environment's magnetic field when they are present. EMF detectors are hand-held meters that measure dips or surges in this field, alerting ghost hunters to a ghostly presence. But if you don't want to shell out the bucks for one of these, then a simple hiking compass will work as well. Hold the compass in the palm of your hand as you walk about. If the needle begins to swing erratically, you may have run into something.

- Infrared thermal scanners are another device used to track ghosts. Much like EMF detectors, thermal scanners measure extreme temperature drops in the environment. These "cold spots," as they're called, are thought to occur when a ghost draws energy from its surroundings in order to manifest itself. This process is believed to create a mass of cold air that can be felt by simply walking through it.

- Digital or standard cassette recorders can be used for note taking, interviewing a witness, or even recording the voices of ghosts—electronic voice phenomena (EVP), as the process has come to be known. It is theorized that, although spirit voices occur at a frequency too low for the human ear to register, they can be captured on audio recorders and then amplified into our range of hearing. When attempting to record EVPs, use a microphone with a wind muffle to cut out some of the background noise. If using a standard cassette recorder, always use new tapes. Never try to record over old tapes. Find a promising spot and begin recording. State your name, the time, and the location for later reference. Then, stepping back a few feet, begin addressing questions to possible ghosts in the area, pausing to give them enough time to respond. Remember, their responses won't be audible. When you're finished, again state your name and the time into the recorder. Later you can replay the tapes, ideally through headphones, listening carefully for responses to your questions.

- Film, VHS, and digital cameras can be used to document the existence of ghosts. Everything from expensive point-and-shoot to cheap disposable cameras has been used with success. The one that's right for you will be decided by your preference and your pocketbook.

Cameras should always be used in conjunction with other verifiers, such as EMF detectors or thermal scanners. This way an innocent camera strap or water vapor isn't mistaken for wayward spirits when the film is developed.

The type of film you use can also make a difference, and ghost hunters rely on everything from expensive infrared to common color film, and some even swear by black and white. Film with speeds of 200 to 400 ASA is normally recommended for inside jobs, while a higher speed 800 ASA should be used outdoors. The camera flash can also make a difference—the stronger the flash, the better.

Recently a debate has arisen over the use of digital cameras. The majority of ghost hunters today find them convenient because the LCD screen allows them to preview the pictures that they take, which can save a lot of money when developing the photos. However, there are some purists in the field who claim that inherent problems in the pixilation process can cause reflective images that can be mistaken for ghost orbs.

- Make sure that you include more batteries, film, and tapes than you think you'll need. There are many reports of ghosts draining the batteries in cameras and recorders when they are present, so have some fresh ones to pop in, just in case.

Many of these items are easy enough to obtain and can be found at most electronics stores. The specialty items, like EMF detectors and thermal scanners, can be purchased through the Internet, but be prepared to pay more when ordering from sites specializing in "ghost hunting equipment." Regardless of the items you choose to work with, realize that your ghost hunting kit should be tailored to suit the investigation you plan to conduct. Some ghost hunters like to be armed to the teeth with equipment and ready for anything, while others prefer a less encumbered approach. Ultimately the decision is yours, but remember that the more you take with you, the more equipment you'll have to lug around all night.

Depending on your methods and preferences, you may want to use the services of an experienced psychic. Many ghost hunters avoid psychics because their results are often mixed and extremely hard to verify. On the other hand, some claim to use them with great success and state that they can provide a wealth of information inaccessible by any other means. If you do decide to work with a psychic, consider using more than one on the same investigation, and provide them with as little information about the site as possible. Bring each onto the site separately and allow them to tour the location, picking up whatever impressions they can. Then compare their findings with one another and with the information that you already have. Over time, a ghost hunter may come to trust one or more psychics and work with them exclusively. Finding an honest, accurate psychic can be a difficult task, and your best bet is to contact other researchers or ghost clubs to learn with whom they are working. However, stay away from individuals who charge for their services or crave media attention. Most likely they won't be much help to you.

Once you have a working knowledge of the tools at your disposal and are familiar with the haunted sites in your area, it's time to choose a site for your very first investigation. Through your initial research, you probably have a sketchy idea of the location, but before you begin you'll need to flesh out the history of the place with as much detail as possible. When gathering this information, keep in mind such questions as who lived or possibly died there, and whether there were traumatic events or other factors that could have led to the place becoming haunted.

If it's a public building or property, the task of gathering information may be much easier, with public records being abundant and easy to obtain. A hunt through the library's local history section could turn up information on both the site and the surrounding area. The Internet can also be of help here, with city and county maps often available online. Larger or older cities may have maps, street by street and house by house, developed over many years. Examining these can show how a property developed over time or how a building or other structure has changed. Most cities and towns also keep yearly directories that contain the names and addresses of people who lived at a given location, as well as how long they owned the property and what their occupations were. As you learn more about the people who once lived there, check the obituaries for death notices or enlist the aid of genealogical groups and historical societies. You may even find documentation of traumatic events such as suicides or murders that happened at the location. Remember that traumatic events can provide clues as to why the place is haunted. Neighbors in the area normally have some gossip about the place and may have known those who once lived there. Although much of their information will be in the form of local legends, they may have witnessed the ghostly manifestations for themselves. Finally, once you discover who the current owners are, call or write a letter requesting information about the place and about any strange events that may have occurred while they have lived there.

After learning all you can about the place, decide if there is enough evidence to pursue an on-site investigation. If not, then move on to another site that holds more promise. But if you're still interested in the site you've researched, contact the current owners and politely request an interview. Some of the people that you contact will be very interested in working with you and sharing their experiences. Having someone sympathetic to what they're going through, if their haunting is active, can be a great relief and it helps to reassure them that they're not just "going crazy." Others, however, either out of skepticism or the desire to preserve their privacy, may refuse your request. If this happens, then be understanding and withdraw gracefully.

If a witness does consent to an interview, there are a number of things to keep in mind before you show up with your recorder and questions. First, contact the witness, set a time and date that is convenient for him or her, and get prior permission to enter the property. A ghost hunter should never trespass on private property. Make sure that you arrive on time and thank them for meeting with you. Always respect their right to confidentiality concerning persons or places, and never bring in third parties like the media or specialists without their consent. If possible, ask them if they will sign an information release form. An example of one can be found at the back of this book in the section on ghost hunting forms.

Conducting an interview can be more difficult than it sounds and requires a certain amount of skill. Consider practicing your questions on friends or fellow ghost hunters to hone your skills. As many reporters and police officials can attest, no two witnesses see the same incident identically and observations can be influenced by many factors, such as religious or cultural beliefs. The way witnesses view the experience can change over time as details are lost from memory or are transformed as they struggle to understand what happened to them. If possible, get a detailed a report as quickly as you can. Have your interviewee walk you through the event at the location where it occurred for better details. Walking through the event can help him or her remember important facts that may have escaped their attention at the time it occurred.

Always maintain a professional and impartial relationship with the witnesses to avoid tainting the interview. This includes being careful not to feed the witnesses additional information during the questioning. Let them tell you their story and try not to fill in the blanks for them. While they're speaking, pay close attention to their personality and surroundings, as these may help determine their credibility as a witness. Sometimes how a person says something is just as important as what he or she says.

The following list is provided to help you understand what types of questions work best during an interview:

What were the exact time, location, and weather conditions during the event?

How did the event occur?

Was there a visual manifestation?

Did the event involve sounds of any kind?

Were there any unusual smells?

During the event, was there a sense of touch or being touched involved?

Were any objects moved?

Did you experience any electrical problems with items?

Were you alone at the time or were others present?

If others were present, did they also witness the event?

How did you feel after the event—scared, confused, excited?

How did you feel both mentally and physically just before the event?

What were you doing just prior to the event—sleeping, reading, watching TV?

The remaining questions should be asked in addition to those above and focus more on the witness rather than his or her encounter. These revealing questions will give you a better understanding of the witness and his or her belief system.

Do you believe in ghosts?

Did you believe in ghosts before the event?

Are you active in a church or religion?

How does your church or religion feel about ghosts and the afterlife?

Did you believe the location was haunted before your encounter with the ghost?

Has anyone close to you recently died?

Are you now, or were you at the time of the event, on medication?

Have you recently been treated for a mental illness?

Were you drinking alcohol near or at the time of the event?

Have you ever been involved in a séance, used a Ouija board, or attempted any other form of communication with spirits?

If so, did it occur at this location?

Have you ever experimented with witchcraft or black magic?

If so, did it occur at this location?

After the interview, review the responses of the witnesses, checking their account against the facts at hand. For instance, if they report it was bright and sunny that day, check the weather report and see if it wasn't raining instead. If others were present, interview them also and compare the reports. It's true that no two accounts will be the same, but major discrepancies should be obvious.

After the interview, you'll have to decide if there's enough evidence of paranormal activity to conduct a vigil. A vigil is often the most exciting part of the investigation and involves teams of ghost hunters staking out a haunted location in order to document the existence of ghosts. Vigils involve a great deal of planning to ensure safe and productive results.

First of all, never conduct a vigil by yourself. No matter how experienced ghost hunters are, they always realize the need for safety. Teams of two or more should be maintained at all times. Notify family and friends before you set out, telling them where you will be and when you expect to be back. In addition, should you be stopped by the police or others wondering what you're doing running around some old house at night with flashlights, carrying proper identification will save you some explaining. Notify the local authorities about the vigil to further guard against interference.

Needless to say, it is never, under any circumstances, acceptable for a ghost hunter to trespass on private property. Always obtain permission from the owners of the property before you begin. Make sure that they are informed in detail about exactly what the investigation will entail, including what equipment you will use, the hours you will be there, and the people involved, to prevent any misunderstandings later. Having the owners sign a consent form giving your group permission to conduct a vigil on the property will help a great deal. Keep this on you at all times in case the police arrive and wonder what's going on. (See an example of a consent form in the section on ghost hunting forms.)

Whether you're a first-time ghost hunter or one with a lot of spooks under your belt, always conduct yourself in a professional manner. That includes no horseplay, alcohol, drugs, or smoking during the vigil. Remember that each site should be treated with a sense of the sacred, befitting a place where people once lived and possibly died. That also means that you are responsible for any damages that occur while you are there.

Before you arrive, make sure that you check all the equipment you plan to use and ensure that there are more than enough batteries, film, and tapes to get you through. Each member of the group should be able to operate every piece of equipment and fully understand what his or her duties will be. Give each person a specific job or function to perform. Practice makes perfect and, after a few dry runs, your group should be able to iron out all the kinks. Also think about the size of the group and try to establish the right number for the job. Too many ghost hunters and they'll be tripping over themselves; not enough and you won't be able to investigate effectively. Usually six is a good number to work with and allows you to break into teams of either twos or threes evenly.

If you're planning to hold a night vigil, then arrive before dusk in order to familiarize the group with the layout. Draw a map marking the location of important objects or landmarks such as windows, lights, trees, depressions or graves, and exits. Photographs taken of each area during the day, especially hot zones of reported activity, can be used as reference points later when it's dark. After everyone knows the grounds and has a copy of the map, establish a base area where unused equipment can be kept and teams can report in or regroup. Keep in mind, however, that although ghost hunting seems natural at night, it's also unnecessary. Ghosts have been known to appear at any hour on any day, regardless of the weather. Vigils can be held during the day as well as at night and thinking otherwise is mere romantic fluff.

Ghost hunters usually plan their vigils using one of three approaches. The one that you choose will depend on several things, including whether it will be held indoors or out, the types of equipment you have access to, and the types of reported manifestations. The easiest approach is to set up your equipment in a hot zone and monitor the results. The sedentary method works particularly well indoors or when the reported manifestations are limited to a certain spot such as a room. However, if the activity is spread out over a larger area like a cemetery, then a roaming approach will work better, with team members patrolling the area with detection equipment. Some situations, though, may call for a mixture of the two in order to cover all the bases. Certain teams can be assigned to known hot zones to monitor for activity while the rest of the group sweeps the surrounding area.

No matter which approach you decide to use, each member of the group should keep a logbook noting details such as time, temperature changes, weather patterns, the phase of the moon, and instrument readings. Each observation, no matter how small it may seem at the time, should be recorded as it occurs. When the logbooks are later compared to one another, they may point to interesting patterns or anomalies overlooked during the vigil. These detailed accounts can also help determine where mistakes were made and what areas could stand improvement. In the end, a carefully maintained logbook can be the most important tool you use as a ghost hunter. An example of one can be found in the section on ghost hunting forms to help you better understand what details of a vigil to record.

As a ghost hunter, there is always the risk that you will find what you are looking for—a ghost. That is, after all, why you're conducting an investigation in the first place, right? Well, when it does happen, you will need to be prepared for the event. This includes staying calm and not running off in pure fright. The first thing you will want to do when confronting an apparition or some other manifestation is to notify the other members in your group using your radio. The greater the number of persons that can witness the manifestation, the better. Multiple witnesses give your sighting more credibility, as well as establish that it's an objective experience and not just some trick of the imagination. You may not have much time, as such encounters are usually very brief, so quickly begin measuring the effects of the manifestation on the environment around you, checking for shifts in the electromagnetic fields or fluctuations in the temperature. If any of these are evident, record them in your logbook and, if possible, collect evidence using your camera or audio recorder. Whatever you do, don't go chasing after the ghost. Experience has proven that sudden movements or noise will cause them to vanish.

The various forms a ghost can take are many, and you should be prepared for each of them. The following are a few of the manifestations that you might experience and some of the ways you should handle them. On a vigil, you may encounter unexplained sounds including raps, booms, footsteps, music, and even disembodied voices. In the history of ghost hunting, everything from full-length conversations with the dead to the sounds of battle between ancient armies has been recorded. If you encounter a manifestation in this form, make sure your tape recorders are rolling and take note of what type of sound it is, how long it lasts, and where it's coming from.

You may also witness objects moving by themselves. These can include just about any item imaginable, from small Lego blocks to heavy pieces of furniture. Ghost hunters have watched objects float across a room or hurtle toward them when their backs were turned, and in some cases items have even dropped from the ceiling as if from thin air. If your investigation involves objects that are prone to moving about, outlining them in chalk will help determine their movements. Keep track of the direction they travel, their speed, distance, and the force it would take to move the object itself. After it has moved, return the item to its original position and examine it for changes.

Odd smells have also been known to occur in connection with ghosts, ranging from appealing scents like perfume or freshly brewed coffee to offensive odors like sour liquor or feces. When a manifestation of this kind occurs, take note of the type of smell you recognize, where it seems to be the strongest, and how long the odor lasts.

There may even be an encounter where you touch or are touched by an unseen presence during the vigil. This experience can take various forms, from a soft comforting embrace to the violence of a slap or push that can leave physical marks afterward. If anything like this happens to you, stay calm and record the experience as best you can. Pay attention to what kind of touch occurred, how long it lasted, and how it made you feel—comforted or threatened. Remember to check your skin for marks left by particularly forceful encounters.

Finally, you may even witness one of the rarest forms of manifestation—an apparition. These can include anything from mist-like clouds to glowing spheres to full or partial human forms. Once again, if you see one, do not attempt to follow. Instead, take as many pictures as you can, paying attention to the apparition's mannerisms, gestures, clothing, and the path that it takes. Some of these clues may later help you to uncover the identity of the ghost and why it's choosing to stick around.

Ideally, ghost hunters limit their vigils to no more than three or four hours. Longer periods have a tendency to wear team members out, causing fatigue or, even worse, boredom. These conditions can deteriorate the quality of observation, and a tired or wandering mind can lead to mistakes resulting in injuries when roaming through a dark cemetery or old house. However, some investigations may call for vigils that last more than just a few hours. In fact, the investigation of Borley Rectory was essentially one long vigil that lasted an entire year. If your vigil promises to be a long one, then consider rotating your teams every two to four hours to keep members fresh and on their toes.

When it's time to end the vigil, make sure that you leave the site exactly as you found it, including picking up any trash left behind. Remember that your group is responsible for any damage that occurs while you are there. How your group behaves on the vigil will determine whether or not you're welcome back again. Property owners who are impressed with your professionalism can act as a great reference for future investigations.

Once you arrive home, let family and friends know that the vigil has ended and that everything went safely. Before too much time has passed, study all of the vigil logs, tapes, and photographs, looking for anything that you may have missed earlier. This can be very time-consuming, with hours and hours of material to study. Have patience and try dividing the material into manageable chunks with enough breaks in between to keep from feeling overwhelmed. This will ensure that nothing important is missed and no evidence is lost or passed over.

Regardless of whether you counted the vigil a success or just a waste of time, consider a follow-up visit to the site. Things may have changed since you were there last and striking out the first time doesn't mean that the site isn't haunted.

A haunting often has the frustrating ability to fluctuate between times of intense activity and complete dormancy spanning many years (hundreds, in some cases). Even worse is a ghost's seemingly natural dislike for being studied and its habit of disappearing whenever ghost hunters are present.

Unfortunately, for all the talk of phantom voices and misty shapes, the fact is that 98 percent of alleged hauntings have a natural explanation. William of Ockham (ca. 1287–1347), a scientist and logician, famously stated, "*Pluralitas non est ponenda sine necessitate*," or when translated into English: "Plurality is not to be posited without necessity." This popular little phrase later became known as Ockham's razor and, paraphrased, means that the simplest explanation is usually the best. All those thumps and bumps in the night could merely be bad plumbing acting up. That woman in white spotted roaming the cemetery could be nothing more than a trick of the moonlight reflecting off tombstones. Therefore, a successful ghost hunter approaches all his or her investigations with an open mind tempered with a bit of skepticism.

If the site involves a house or other structure, try contacting plumbers, builders, and electricians to inquire whether any of the manifestations reported might have natural explanations. For instance, lights going on and off by themselves may be evidence of a playful spirit or it may be merely bad wiring, something not unheard of in older homes. If these professionals cannot shed any light on the phenomena, they can still give you some good advice on where to start looking. You can also try discovering whether the house sits over an underground water source, cave system, or abandoned mine-shaft, which can cause it to settle oddly, resulting in strange noises and moving objects. Keep in mind too that many older homes are inhabited by more than just human occupants, including birds, mice, squirrels, and raccoons. Once lodged in the walls and ceilings, these critters can make some un-usual noises at night. That nocturnal ghost blundering about your home in the late hours opening cabinets may be noth-ing more than a pesky raccoon looking for a midnight snack. Finally, the effects of the weather should be taken into ac-count, too. A psychic cold spot could actually be the result of a chilling draft, or an eerie phantom figure may be just a com-bination of mist and moonlight. Many of these conditions, coupled with poor observation and a bit of imagination, can lead to some startling and rather scary encounters. During an investigation, a ghost hunter should strive to exhaust all the natural explanations before turning to spirits for answers.

There is one final factor to consider when explaining a haunting: are parts of it, or even all of it, being faked? Sadly, this is a question that every ghost hunter must consider while investigating a case. Understanding why someone would fake a haunting will help understand how to spot one. There are two primary reasons why a person or persons would be involved in such a deception: for the attention or for the simple thrill of it. Publicity can add up to big bucks in some cases, with book deals and movies just waiting to be made. A good old-fashioned haunting can also draw in money-spending customers, and many restaurants and bed and breakfasts boast a ghost or two as part of their appeal.

Ghost hunters should always ask themselves what the motivations of the witnesses are and whether they stand to gain anything through a haunting. There are also those individuals who simply love the attention of it all. Even the great Spiritualist movement of the nineteenth century was said to have been sparked by two small children with an apple on a string, scaring their mother for a bit of fun. Keep in mind that children are not the only offenders and even adults have been caught red-handed.

Unless you catch someone in the act with a bedsheet over his head, rattling chains and going "boo," smoking out fraud can be very difficult. There are some signs, however, that should send out warning signals when you run across them. These may include witnesses who are overly enthusiastic about events, who show a lack of fright over what they have just experienced, or who try hard to influence the ghost hunter. In addition, beware of statements that fall outside the pattern of a normal haunting or are made by one member of the household while others report little or no activity. In instances where there is more than one witness, always interview each separately to see if their accounts match up. The world is full of people who love a good joke, so listen to your instincts and, if you suspect someone of faking a haunting, don't waste your breath confronting them. Simply move on to other prospects that better deserve your attention.

For some, ghost hunting is an interesting hobby—a pastime that provides a few thrills and chills on a late Saturday night. For others, it's a passion for the mystery that itches away just under the surface, waiting to be solved. Whether you're just beginning as a ghost hunter or you have been at it for some time, the suggestions in this chapter will help you stay safe and have fun. As new ghost hunters enter the field, they bring with them a unique blend of talents, beliefs, and approaches. There are no hard and fast rules to ghost hunting that will make it easy for you, but by studying the ghost hunters that came before, you can keep from making the same mistakes.

We've talked a lot in this chapter about ghosts, hauntings, and ghost hunting, but unfortunately these terms have the ability to diminish the importance of the event. The entities that you seek are not a collection of generic words stuck in a book. They are somebody's mother, brother, or grandparent. The site you walk on is a place where they lived, died, or were buried. They deserve our utmost respect, and the ground we tread on, which they once walked themselves, is sacred. Each ghost, each haunting, has a story to tell, a story about what it means to be human. If we come with respect and curiosity, if we come and we listen quietly, these ghosts will tell us their tale.

Ghost Hunting Forms

These forms may be of some use to those attempting a ghost hunt of their very own. Realize that each situation is unique and that anyone using these forms may feel the need to change them to meet their particular needs. Please think of them as guidelines or templates when considering what type of information is necessary in making forms of your own.

Release of Information and Evidence

I, _____, would like to use
some or all of the information and evidence collected
during the investigation for possible publication or
other media considerations. In order to respect your
right to privacy, all information given by you will be
confidential unless otherwise noted below.

____ You may release information and evidence,
      providing the identities of the witnesses are pro-
      tected and the address of the location is excluded.

____ You may release all of the information and evi-
      dence collected during the investigation.

____ Further comments or requests:

_____

_____

_____

_____

Signed _____ Date: _____

Witness _____ Date: _____

Investigation Permission Form

I, _____, have the authority to allow access to the present persons for the purpose of conducting an investigation at the following location:

_____

_____

The investigation has been explained to me and I give the research team permission to conduct the investigation at this location.

The members of the research team release the owner of the location from any liability for any injuries or damages that may occur during the investigation. Further, the research team takes full responsibility for any damages to the property during the investigation.

Signed _____ Date: _____

Witness _____ Date: _____

Ghost Hunter's Log

Date: _____ Time Started: _____

Investigator: _____

Site Location: _____

_____

Weather Conditions: _____

_____

Team Members Present:

_____

_____

_____

Equipment Being Used:

_____

_____

_____

Time Finished: _____

Phenomena Witnessed

Time   Phenomenon

_____   _____

_____   _____

_____   _____

_____   _____

_____   _____

_____   _____

_____   _____

_____   _____

_____   _____

Additional Notes: _____

_____

_____

Investigator's Initials: _____

Suggested Readings

The following are a few books on the subject of ghosts that you might find enjoyable. To list all of the wonderful works written on the subject is beyond the scope of this book; however, those below are worth exploring for the diehard ghost hunter as well as those of you who just love a good story.

The Amityville Horror by Jay Anson

Animal Ghosts by Raymond Bayless

Apparitions and Survival of Death by Raymond Bayless

The Case for Ghosts: An Objective Look at the Paranormal by J. Allan Danelek

Complete Idiot's Guide to Ghosts and Hauntings by Tom Ogden

Confessions of a Ghost Hunter by Harry Price

Deathbed Visions by Sir William Barrett

Encyclopedia of Ghosts by Daniel Cohen

Encyclopedia of Ghosts and Spirits by Rosemary Ellen Guiley

The Enigma of the Poltergeist by Raymond Bayless

An Experience of Phantoms by D. Scott Rogo

The Ghost Hunter's Guide by Peter Underwood

The Ghost Hunter's Guidebook by Troy Taylor

The Ghost of Flight 401 by John G. Fuller

Halloween and Other Festivals of Death and Life edited by Jack Santino

Haunted Places: The National Directory by Dennis William Hauck

Here, Mr. Splitfoot by Robert Somerlott

The Heyday of Spiritualism by Slater Brown

How to Be a Ghost Hunter by Richard Southall

The Life and Many Deaths of Harry Houdini by Ruth Brandon

Lord Halifax's Ghost Book: A Collection of Stories of Haunted Houses, Apparitions, and Supernatural Occurrences Made by Charles Lindley, Viscount Halifax by Charles Lindley

Mediums of the 19th Century by Frank Podmore

The Most Haunted House in England by Harry Price

Nights in Haunted Houses by Peter Underwood

Paranormal Investigator's Handbook by Valerie Hope and
Maurice Townsend

Phantasms of the Living by Edmund Gurney, Frank
Podmore, and Frederic Myers

The Poltergeist Experience by D. Scott Rogo

Poltergeist Over England by Harry Price

Poltergeist! A Study in Destructive Haunting by Colin
Wilson

Real Ghosts, Restless Spirits, and Haunted Places by Brad
Steiger

Table-Rappers by Ronald Pearsall

True Hauntings: Spirits with a Purpose by Hazel M.
Denning

RELATED ORGANIZATIONS
AND WEB SITES

Included in this section are several organizations dedicated to the pursuit of education, research, and documentation of ghosts. The following are those in their field who have proven over the years both their sincerity and their professionalism. These are a great source of information and a place to find others with an interest in ghosts. The information provided comes directly from the Web site of each organization, and it is strongly suggested that you consider visiting them to learn more. Without the invaluable contribution of such groups, the subject of ghosts and apparitions would be nothing more than mere superstition.

American Ghost Society
1515 East Third Street
Alton, IL 62002
www.prairieghosts.com

> The American Ghost Society is a national network of ghost hunters and researchers dedicated to finding haunted locations and assisting those who find themselves experiencing a haunting. They do not work with psychics and

maintain a strict set of standards during each investigation. The AGS provides a newsletter and private discussion board for members on its Web site, as well as access to ghost hunting courses and equipment.

American Society for Psychical Research, Inc.
5 West 73rd Street
New York, NY 10023
www.aspr.com

The American Society for Psychical Research is the oldest organization of its kind here in the United States. Founded in 1885, the ASPR was created to support the scientific investigation of the extraordinary and unexplained. It currently maintains laboratories, offices, and a library system that includes rare books, case reports, letters, and manuscripts, some of which date back as far as the 1700s. Its membership is international and boasts some of the greatest thinkers of our time.

Committee for the Scientific Investigation of Claims of the Paranormal
Box 703
Amherst, NY 14226
www.csicop.org

The Committee for the Scientific Investigation of Claims of the Paranormal was created to investigate claims of the paranormal relying solely on the tools of science. The CSICOP funds research programs to investigate paranormal claims, as well as provides a network of information sharing between researchers. The organization also publishes a periodical and has an excellent Web site geared toward those approaching the subject from a critically objective point of view. The CSICOP is definitely the place if you consider yourself a diehard skeptic.

New England Society for Psychical Research
P.O. Box 41
Monroe, CT 06468
www.warrens.net

The New England Society for Psychical Research was founded by famed ghost hunters Ed and Lorraine Warren in 1952. The purpose of the society is to investigate hauntings and other unexplained activities in both the United States and Europe. The NESPR provides communication and understanding of the field through their Web site publication *The Journal*, membership meetings, and classes.

International Ghost Hunters Society
www.ghostweb.com

The International Ghost Hunters Society is committed to the education, research, and investigation of ghosts and apparitions. The society claims a worldwide membership of more than fourteen thousand in eighty-seven countries. Their Web site provides information, a large archive of ghost photos, membership information, ghost hunting equipment, and classes. The IGHS prides itself on its investigative protocols and the fact that membership into the society is free. All you need to be a member is a love for ghosts.

The Society for Psychical Research
49 Marloes Road
Kensington, London W8 6LA
www.spr.ac.uk

The Society for Psychical Research was founded in 1882 by a group of distinguished Cambridge scholars. As the first such organization of its kind, the SPR has been a pioneer in the field of psychical research by promoting and sponsoring important scientific research. Its members continue to influence the study of psychical research through publication of scholarly reports and educational activities.

Bibliography

Bayless, Raymond. *Animal Ghosts*. New York: University Books, 1970.

Bettenson, Henry. *Documents of the Christian Church*. London: Oxford University Press, 1954.

Brandon, Ruth. *The Life and Many Deaths of Harry Houdini*. New York: Random House, 1993.

Chambers, Paul. *Paranormal People: The Famous, the Infamous and the Supernatural*. London: Blandford, 1999.

Cohen, Daniel. *The Encyclopedia of Ghosts*. New York: Dorset Press, 1984.

Crookes, Sir William. *Crookes and the Spirit World: A Collection of Writings by or Concerning the Work of Sir William Crookes, O.M., F.R.S., in the Field of Psychical Research*. New York: Taplinger Co., 1972.

David-Néel, Alexandra. *Magic and Mystery in Tibet*. New York: Dover Publications, 1971.

Denning, Hazel M. *True Hauntings: Spirits with a Purpose*. St. Paul, MN: Llewellyn, 1996.

Edmunds, Simeon. *Spiritualism: A Critical Survey*. London: Aquarian Press, 1966.

Gardner, John, John R. Maier, and Richard A. Henshaw. *Gilgamesh: Translated from the Sin-lequ-unninni Version*. New York: Knopf, 1984.

Gauld, Alan. *The Founders of Psychical Research*. New York: Schocken Books, 1968.

Grant, James. *The Mysteries of All Nations: Rise and Progress of Superstition, Laws Against and Trials of Witches, Ancient and Modern Delusions; Together with Strange Customs, Fables, and Tales*. Detroit: Gale Research Co., 1971.

Guiley, Rosemary Ellen. *The Encyclopedia of Ghosts and Spirits*. New York: Facts on File, 1992.

Gurney, Edmund and Eleanor Mildred Sidgwick. *Phantasms of the Living: Cases of Telepathy Printed in the Journal of the Society for Psychical Research during Thirty-Five Years*. New Hyde Park, NY: University Books, 1962.

Gurney, Edmund, Frederic Myers, and Frank Podmore. *Phantasms of the Living*. Gainesville, FL: Scholars' Facsims. & Reprints, 1970.

Hamilton-Paterson, James, and Carol Andrews. *Mummies: Death and Life in Ancient Egypt*. London: Collins [for] British Museum Publications Ltd., 1978.

Harris, Melvin. *Investigating the Unexplained*. Buffalo, NY: Prometheus Books, 1986.

Hines, Terence. *Pseudoscience and the Paranormal: A Critical Examination of the Evidence.* Buffalo, NY: Prometheus Books, 1988.

King, Francis. *Wisdom from Afar.* Garden City, NY: Doubleday, 1975.

Mackenzie, Andrew. *Apparitions and Ghosts.* London: Barker, 1971.

Moody, Raymond. *Life After Life: The Investigation of a Phenomenon—Survival of Bodily Death.* Harrisburg, PA: Stackpole Books, 1976.

Myers, Arthur. *The Ghosthunter's Guide to Haunted Landmarks, Parks, Churches, and Other Public Places.* Chicago: Contemporary Books, 1993.

Nelson, Geoffrey K. *Spiritualism and Society.* New York: Schocken Books, 1969.

Osborn, Arthur Walter. *The Meaning of Personal Existence in the Light of Paranormal Phenomena, the Doctrine of Reincarnation, and Mystical States of Consciousness.* Wheaton, IL: Theosophical Pub. House, 1967.

Ostrander, Sheila, and Lynn Schroeder. *Psychic Discoveries Behind the Iron Curtain.* Englewood Cliffs, NJ: Prentice-Hall, 1970.

The Pharsalia of Lucan. As translated by Sir Edward Ridley. London: Longmans, Green, and Co., 1896.

Price, Harry. *Confessions of a Ghost Hunter.* New York: Causeway Books, 1974.

———. *The Most Haunted House in England: Ten Years'
Investigation of Borley Rectory.* Alexandria, VA: Time-Life
Books, 1990.

Rogo, D. Scott. *An Experience of Phantoms.* New York: Taplinger Pub. Co., 1974.

———. *In Search of the Unknown: The Odyssey of a Psychical
Investigator.* New York: Taplinger Pub. Co., 1976.

Santino, Jack, editor. *Halloween and Other Festivals of Death
and Life.* Knoxville: University of Tennessee Press, 1994.

Silverman, Kenneth. *Houdini! The Career of Ehrich Weiss.*
New York: HarperCollins Publishers, 1996.

Stirling, A. M. W. *Ghosts Vivisected: An Impartial Inquiry into
Their Manners, Habits, Mentality, Motives and Physical Con-
struction.* New York: Citadel Press, 1958.

Syers, W. C. and William Edward Syers. *Ghost Stories of Texas.*
Waco, TX: Texian Press, 1981.

Taylor, Troy. *The Ghost Hunter's Guidebook: The Essential
Handbook of Ghost Research.* Alton, IL: Whitechapel Pro-
ductions Press, 2001.

Vandenberg, Philipp. *The Mystery of the Oracles: World-
Famous Archaeologists Reveal the Best-Kept Secrets of Antiq-
uity.* New York: Macmillan, 1982.

Ward, Anne G. *Adventures in Archaeology.* New York:
Larousse & Company, Inc., 1977.

Warren, Ed, Lorraine Warren, and Robert David Chase. *Ghost Hunters: True Stories from the World's Most Famous Demonologists.* New York: St. Martin's Press, 1989.

Warren, Ed, and Lorraine Warren. *Graveyard: True Hauntings from an Old New England Cemetery.* New York: St. Martin's Press, 1992.

Whitaker, Terence W. *Haunted England: Royal Spirits, Castle Ghosts, Phantom Coaches & Wailing Ghouls.* Chicago: Contemporary Books, 1987.

Wilson, Colin. *Poltergeist! A Study in Destructive Haunting.* London: Caxton Editions, 2001.

Wolman, Benjamin B. *Handbook of Parapsychology.* New York: Van Nostrand Reinhold, 1977.

Free Catalog

Get the latest information on our body, mind, and spirit products! To receive a **free** copy of Llewellyn's consumer magazine, *New Worlds of Mind & Spirit,* simply call 1-877-NEW-WRLD or visit our website at www.llewellyn.com and click on *New Worlds*.

☾ LLEWELLYN ORDERING INFORMATION

Order Online:
Visit our website at www.llewellyn.com, select your books, and order them on our secure server.

Order by Phone:
- Call toll-free within the U.S. at 1-877-NEW-WRLD (1-877-639-9753). Call toll-free within Canada at 1-866-NEW-WRLD (1-866-639-9753)
- We accept VISA, MasterCard, and American Express

Order by Mail:
Send the full price of your order (MN residents add 6.5% sales tax) in U.S. funds, plus postage & handling to:

> **Llewellyn Worldwide**
> **2143 Wooddale Drive, Dept. 978-0-7387-1363-2**
> **Woodbury, MN 55125-2989, U.S.A.**

Postage & Handling:

Standard (U.S., Mexico, & Canada). If your order is:
$24.99 and under, add $3.00
$25.00 and over, FREE STANDARD SHIPPING

AK, HI, PR: $15.00 for one book plus $1.00 for each additional book.

International Orders (airmail only):
$16.00 for one book plus $3.00 for each additional book

Orders are processed within 2 business days.
Please allow for normal shipping time. Postage and handling rates subject to change.

How to Be a Ghost Hunter
RICHARD SOUTHALL

So you want to investigate a haunting? This book is full of practical advice used in the author's own ghost- hunting practice. Find out whether you're dealing with a ghost, spirit, or an entity . . . and discover the one time when you should stop what you're doing and call in an exorcist. Learn the four-phase procedure for conducting an effective investigation, how to capture paranormal phenomena on film, record disembodied sounds and voices on tape, assemble an affordable ghost-hunting kit, and form your own paranormal group.

For anyone with time and little money to spend on equipment, this book will help you maintain a healthy sense of skepticism and thoroughness while you search for authentic evidence of the paranormal.

978-0-7387-0312-1
168 pp., 5³⁄₁₆ x 8, photos   **$12.95**

Spanish edition:
Espíritus y fantasmas
978-0-7387-0382-4   **$12.95**

Ghost Worlds

*A Guide to Poltergeists, Portals,
Ecto-Mist & Spirit Behavior*

MELBA GOODWYN

From communicating with spirits to witnessing orbs burst from an inter-dimensional portal, Melba Goodwyn has seen it all as a psychic spirit investigator. In this fascinating examination of paranormal phenomena, she offers original insights into the nature of ghosts and haunting, true stories of her thrilling adventures, and practical ghost hunting tips.

How are traditional ghosts different from poltergeists? How does a place or an object become haunted? What are orbs, ecto-mist, vortexes, and energy anomalies? Goodwyn defines different kinds of ghosts and entities, how they manifest, and why they are attracted to certain places.

978-0-7387-1195-9
264 pp., 5³/₁₆ x 8 $14.95

True Hauntings

Spirits with a Purpose

HAZEL M. DENNING, PH.D.

How do ghosts feel and think? Do they suffer? Does death automatically promote them to a paradise, or as some believe, a hell? In *True Hauntings*, psychic researcher Dr. Hazel M. Denning recounts the real-life case histories of the earthbound spirits—both benevolent and malevolent—she has investigated. She also explores spirit possession, psychic attack, mediumship, and spirit guides.

978-1-56718-218-7
240 pp., 6 x 9 $12.95

To order, call 1-877-NEW-WRLD

House of Spirits and Whispers

The True Story of a Haunted House

Annie Wilder

Annie Wilder suspected the funky 100-year-old house was haunted when she saw it for the first time. But nothing could have prepared her for the mischievous and downright scary antics that take place once she and her family move in. Disembodied conversation, pounding walls, glowing orbs, and mysterious whispers soon escalate into full-fledged ghostly visits. Determined to make peace with her spirit guests, she invites renowned clairvoyant Echo Bodine over and learns fascinating details about each of the entities residing there.

Wilder's gripping tale provides a compelling glimpse into the otherworldly nature of the lonely spirits, protective forces, phantom pets, and departed loved ones that occupy her remarkable home.

978-0-7387-0777-8
192 pp., 6 x 9   **$12.95**

Spanish edition:
Ecos y susurros de una casa embrujada
978-0-7387-0910-9   **$12.95**

To order, call 1-877-NEW-WRLD
Prices subject to change without notice

To Write to the Author

If you wish to contact the author or would like more information about this book, please write to the author in care of Llewellyn Worldwide and we will forward your request. Both the author and publisher appreciate hearing from you and learning of your enjoyment of this book and how it has helped you. Llewellyn Worldwide cannot guarantee that every letter written to the author can be answered, but all will be forwarded. Please write to:

Brian Righi
℅ Llewellyn Worldwide
2143 Wooddale Drive, Dept. 978-0-7387-1363-2
Woodbury, MN 55125-2989, U.S.A.

Please enclose a self-addressed stamped envelope for reply,
or $1.00 to cover costs. If outside U.S.A., enclose
international postal reply coupon.

Many of Llewellyn's authors have websites with additional information and resources. For more information, please visit our website at:

www.llewellyn.com